# 区域国别学概论

*Introduction to Area Studies*

主　编　朱殿勇　车德伟
副主编　张俊南　杨　剑

哈爾濱工程大學出版社
Harbin Engineering University Press

## 内容简介

在全球化退潮与地缘裂变的时代，区域国别学作为新兴交叉学科对于理解、研究地缘政治、经济与文化互动至关重要。本书聚焦全球不同地区与文化的复杂性，剖析其独特特征及当代议题。

本书理论框架体系层次分明，内容编排多维化，知识整合结构化。首先，介绍区域国别研究的学科起源、发展历程及学术意义；其次，阐述相关理论与方法论框架，为读者提供研究工具；最后，扩展至全球视野，涵盖欧洲一体化进程、海洋与技术的战略角色，以及全球治理的基础概念。核心章节聚焦具体案例分析，分别探讨俄罗斯、美国和英国的政治、社会、经济及文化语境，揭示其区域特殊性。本书通过多维度解析，助力读者深入理解区域多样性及其全球关联性。

本书可作为相关专业学生的专业教材，也可作为相关研究人员的参考用书。

**图书在版编目(CIP)数据**

区域国别学概论 / 朱殿勇, 车德伟主编. -- 哈尔滨 : 哈尔滨工程大学出版社, 2025. 8. -- ISBN 978-7-5661-4960-2

Ⅰ. D81

中国国家版本馆 CIP 数据核字第 2025NT2406 号

**区域国别学概论**
QUYUGUOBIEXUE GAILUN

**选题策划** 刘凯元
**责任编辑** 田雨虹
**封面设计** 李海波

**出版发行** 哈尔滨工程大学出版社
**社　　址** 哈尔滨市南岗区南通大街 145 号
**邮政编码** 150001
**电　　话** 0451-82519989
**经　　销** 新华书店
**印　　刷** 哈尔滨市海德利商务印刷有限公司
**开　　本** 787 mm×1 092 mm　1/16
**印　　张** 11.5
**字　　数** 289 千字
**版　　次** 2025 年 8 月第 1 版
**印　　次** 2025 年 8 月第 1 次印刷
**书　　号** ISBN 978-7-5661-4960-2
**定　　价** 56.00 元

http://www.hrbeupress.com
E-mail:heupress@hrbeu.edu.cn

# PREFACE

*Introduction to Area Studies* is a textbook specially edited to provide students and scholars with an essential understanding of the field of area studies. This discipline is a fascinating and dynamic area of study that seeks to explore the complexities of different regions and cultures around the world, offering insights into the unique characteristics and contemporary issues that shape these areas.

In today's increasingly interconnected and globalized world, the importance of area studies cannot be overstated. As we navigate a landscape where regional dynamics influence global politics, economics, and cultural exchanges, a deep and nuanced understanding of different regions becomes essential. This textbook aims to equip readers with the tools and knowledge necessary to engage with and analyze the diverse regions that make up our global community.

The structure of this textbook is designed to provide a balanced and holistic vista to area studies. We begin with an exploration of area studies as a discipline, delving into its origins, evolution, and significance. This foundational unit sets the stage for a deeper dive into the theoretical and methodological frameworks that underpin area studies, helping readers understand the approaches and techniques used by scholars in this field.

Following this, we move into a series of case studies that examine regions as contexts. Units 3, 4, and 5 focus on Russia, the United States, and the United Kingdom, respectively. The three units provide in-depth analyses of these regions, highlighting their unique political, social, economical, and cultural contexts. Through these case studies, readers will gain a deeper appreciation for the complexities and nuances that define each region.

In the latter part of the textbook, we broaden our scope to explore regions within a global context. Units 6, 7, and 8 examine the unification of Europe, the significance of oceans and technology in line with our university's specialized programs, and the fundamentals of global governance.

This textbook is the result of the collaborative efforts of four dedicated editors, each of whom has taken primary responsibility for compiling specific chapters, ensuring that the selected materials are well-represented and thoroughly explored.

We intend to show every respect for intellectual property rights, and hope our pleading for the permission to use the related materials for teaching purposes will receive kind and generous consideration. We hope that this textbook will serve as a valuable resource for students and scholars alike.

# 目录
## CONTENTS

# Unit 1 Area Studies as a Discipline

> To truly grasp the complexities of our globalized world, we must engage deeply with the specificities of different regions.
>
> —John Ikenberry

## LEARNING OUTCOMES

■ Describe the development of Area Studies, including its historical growth, current state, and the impact of China's rising global influence on the field.

■ Evaluate the impact of new technologies on Area Studies research, including digital humanities approaches and big data analytics.

■ Discuss the challenge of balancing deep regional knowledge with global relevance in Area Studies.

■ Assess the role of Area Studies in contributing regional perspectives to global policy discussions, including conflict resolution and cultural diplomacy.

■ Analyze the efforts of Chinese institutions to develop their own Area Studies programs, particularly in the context of China's growing international engagement and the government's emphasis on building global expertise.

## BEFORE CLASS

■ Fareed Zakaria. *The Post American World*(Second Edition). WW Norton, 2012.

■ Samuel P. Huntington. *The Clash of Civilizations and the Remaking of World Order*. Simon & Schuster, 2007.

After you read the above materials, please answer the following questions.

(1) How does Zakaria's concept of the "rise of the rest" challenge traditional notions of American dominance in international relations? What evidence does he provide to support this shift in global power dynamics?

(2) How might Huntington's emphasis on civilizational identities and conflicts challenge traditional Area Studies frameworks based on nation-states or geographic

regions? What are the implications of this civilizational paradigm for understanding regional dynamics and interactions?

(3) Both authors highlight the complex interplay between globalization, economic development, and cultural identity. How might this interplay shape social and political dynamics within and across different world regions, and what are the potential implications for Area Studies scholarship?

(4) Zakaria's and Huntington's books have been influential in shaping public and policy debates about global affairs. What are the implications of this influence for Area Studies scholars, and how might they engage with these broader debates while maintaining academic rigor and nuance?

## 1.1 Introduction to Area Studies and Its Relationship with International Relations

### 1.1.1 Defining Area Studies

Area Studies is an interdisciplinary field that involves the comprehensive study of specific geographical regions, countries or cultures. It integrates perspectives from various social science and humanities disciplines—such as history, political science, economics, anthropology, sociology, and language and cultural studies to develop in-depth knowledge about a particular area. Area Studies differs from traditional disciplines in its explicit focus on geographically bounded spaces and its commitment to integrating multiple disciplinary approaches to understand the historical trajectories, socio-cultural dynamics, political systems, economic systems, and international interactions characterizing those spaces. Rather than seeking to develop universal theories, Area Studies values context-specific knowledge generated through immersive language training, fieldwork, and close engagement with local sources and perspectives.

### 1.1.2 The Interdisciplinary Nature of Area Studies

A defining feature of Area Studies is its interdisciplinarity. Scholars in Area Studies draw upon theories, methods, and insights from a range of social science and humanities fields to develop a holistic understanding of a region. For example, understanding contemporary political dynamics in the Middle East requires attention to the region's history, cultural and religious traditions, social structures, economic conditions, and international relations. An Area Studies approach would seek to integrate knowledge from political science, history, anthropology, economics, religious studies, and other fields to analyze how these multiple factors interact to shape outcomes of interest. This interdisciplinary orientation distinguishes Area Studies from more discipline-bound fields like political science or economics that tend to focus on a narrower set of variables and prioritize abstract theoretical modeling over contextual nuance. The value of Area Studies' interdisciplinary approach lies in its ability to capture the complex, multifaceted nature of real-world regional dynamics that rarely conform to the boundaries of academic disciplines.

### 1.1.3 Area Studies and International Relations: An Overview

The relationship between Area Studies and International Relations (IR) has historically been characterized by tensions and debates over the relative importance of regional expertise versus theoretical generalizability. IR as a field has traditionally sought to develop universal theories to explain patterns of conflict, cooperation, and power dynamics in the international system. From this view, Area Studies, with its emphasis on the particularity of regional contexts, were often seen as atheoretical and lacking in disciplinary rigor. However, there is growing recognition of the value of Area Studies knowledge for informing and refining IR theories and for providing essential context to understand the practical conduct of foreign policy and international affairs. As the international system becomes more multipolar and regionalized, IR must engage with the kinds of localized knowledge that Area Studies produces. At the same time, IR theories offer important frameworks for Area Studies scholars to situate their regional insights within broader global patterns and processes. Concepts like balance of power, security dilemmas, interdependence, norms, and identity from IR theory can help structure comparative analysis across regions and link regional dynamics to system-level variables. Some key areas of potential synergy between Area Studies and IR include the following.

- The interaction between regional orders and global power structures.
- The role of regions and regional powers in shaping global governance.

- The diffusion and localization of transnational norms at regional levels.
- The impact of global economic and security trends on regional stability.
- Regional conflict formations and their management through international institutions.

Engaging these issues productively requires combining IR's theoretical tools with Area Studies' empirical and contextual sensitivity in a two-way dialogue. The following sections explore how this dialogue has evolved and where it may be headed.

APPLY YOUR KNOWLEDGE

1. How might the interdisciplinary nature of Area Studies contribute to a more comprehensive understanding of complex regional issues, such as the ongoing tensions in the Middle East or the economic development of Southeast Asia?

2. How might the integration of Area Studies and IR contribute to more effective foreign policy decision-making? Provide an example of a current international issue where this integrated approach could be beneficial.

## 1.2 Historical Development of Area Studies

The field of Area Studies, which involves the comprehensive, interdisciplinary study of specific geographical regions, countries, or cultures, has a complex history shaped by geopolitical events, intellectual trends, and institutional developments over the past century. While precursors can be traced back further, area studies as a distinct academic field emerged in the early to mid-20th century, particularly in the United States. Its trajectory has been marked by changing rationales, shifting institutional support, and ongoing debates over its relationship to the traditional disciplines.

### 1.2.1 Origins of Area Studies in the Early 20th Century

The roots of area studies lie in the late 19th and early 20th centuries, a period of expanding European and American political and economic influence globally. As the United States began to take on a larger role in world affairs, there was a growing recognition among scholars, policymakers, and philanthropic foundations of the need for more specialized knowledge about foreign regions and cultures. Some early precursors to

Area Studies can be found in the work of geographers like Alexander von Humboldt, who emphasized the comprehensive study of specific regions, and in Orientalist scholarship on Asia and the Middle East, though the latter was often tied to colonial agendas. In the United States, a key early development was the establishment of the first professorship in Chinese language and literature at Yale University in 1877. By 1920, a dozen American universities were offering courses in Chinese language. The interwar period saw the emergence of the first interdisciplinary area studies programs in the United States. In the 1920s and 1930s, programs focusing on regions like Latin America, East Asia, and the Middle East began to be established at major universities with support from the Carnegie and Rockefeller foundations. These early programs combined language training with study of the history, politics, and cultures of their respective regions. A key rationale for these early area studies initiatives was the perceived need for the United States, as an emerging global power, to build up a pool of regional experts. As one report from the Social Science Research Council put it in 1947, the United States lacked the "regional specialists with knowledge of those regions that became of increasing strategic importance" compared to European colonial powers that had built up expertise over centuries. Area studies was seen as a way to fill this knowledge gap. At the same time, area studies in this early period rested on an epistemological claim about the importance of understanding cultural and historical specificity. As Leonard Binder argued, the justification for geographically-focused studies was the idea that "there are very significant differences among peoples and cultures" and therefore "what we know about ourselves is an inadequate basis for understanding others". In this view, area-specific knowledge was essential for challenging ethnocentric assumptions and universalist theories in the social sciences.

### 1.2.2 Impact of World War Ⅱ and the Cold War

While Area Studies began to emerge in the interwar years, it was World War Ⅱ and the early Cold War that catalyzed the field's rapid growth and institutionalization, particularly in the United States. With the U. S. engaged globally in an ideological and geopolitical struggle against communism, area expertise came to be seen as a vital national resource. The war years saw the establishment of crash language and area training programs to serve military and intelligence needs, such as the Army Specialized Training Program. After the war, the U. S. government and major foundations poured substantial resources into building up area studies infrastructure in universities. A major boost came with the *National Defense Education Act of 1958*, spurred by concerns about Soviet scientific advances in the wake of the Sputnik launch. The National Defense Education Act (NDEA) provided funding for university-based area studies centers, known as National Resource Centers, as well as for language training and research. Over the next decade, area studies programs proliferated across the country. For example, by 1970s, there were over 50 East Asian studies centers at American universities. Similar growth occurred for other regions like Latin America, Africa, and the Middle East. Area studies became a major presence in American higher education, supported by a combination of government, foundation, and university funding. The Cold War context shaped area studies in multiple ways. Geopolitically, it made knowledge of world regions, especially those seen as strategically important battlegrounds like Southeast Asia, a priority. Theoretically and methodologically, much area studies scholarship in the 1950s and 1960s was influenced by the dominant paradigm of modernization theory, which posited a universal trajectory from tradition to modernity and was often enlisted to support U. S. foreign policy goals. For example, scholars like Walt Rostow applied modernization frameworks to study economic and political development in regions like Latin America and Southeast Asia, generating knowledge aimed at countering communist influence. The behavioral revolution in political science also pushed area studies in a more quantitative, theory-oriented direction as part of efforts to make the field more "scientific". At the same time, the Cold War era also saw challenges to these paradigms emerge from within area studies. Dependency theory, world-systems analysis, and Neo-Marxist approaches offered critical alternatives to modernization theory, drawing attention to global inequalities and the impact of colonialism and capitalism on the developing world. Scholars like Andre Gunder Frank in Latin American studies and Immanuel Wallerstein in African studies were influential figures. The Vietnam War was a pivotal event that sparked a wave of critical reflection in area studies and the social sciences more broadly. The war, and the role some area experts had played in shaping U. S. policy, led to a crisis of confidence in the field and a questioning of its relationship to government priorities. The publication of Edward Said's *Orientalism* in 1978, though focused on Middle East studies, catalyzed a broader critique of area studies' complicity with imperial power structures and its tendency to exoticize and essentialize other cultures.

## 1.2.3 Critiques and Challenges to Traditional Area Studies

In the wake of the Vietnam War and Orientalism debate, area studies went through a period of soul-searching and transformation. The 1970s and 1980s saw the field grapple with a series of critiques and challenges to its traditional intellectual foundations and institutional structures. Intellectually, area studies was criticized from a number of angles. Disciplinary social scientists argued that its emphasis on descriptive, idiographic knowledge of particular places was a barrier to the development of general theories and models. The privileging of deep, contextual understanding over theoretical generalization was seen by some as perpetuating a problematic divide between nomothetic "scientific" knowledge and idiographic "humanistic" knowledge. Others, drawing on Said's critique, saw area studies as irredeemably tainted by its origins in the age of empire and the Cold War. They argued that the way area studies constructed and represented its objects of study—the "Third World", the "Orient", and the "developing countries", that reflected and reproduced unequal power relations between the West and the rest. Some called for a complete overhaul of the field and a shift towards new paradigms like postcolonial studies. Even among those committed to area studies, there were debates about the continued viability of its traditional regional frameworks in an era of globalization. The idea of studying the world in terms of relatively bounded, self-contained "areas" seemed increasingly out of step with the transnational flows of people, capital, and ideas that were reshaping the global landscape. Some called for a rethinking of area studies around new spatial frames like "the Pacific Rim" or "the Black Atlantic". Institutionally, area studies also faced a number of challenges starting in the 1970s. Government and foundation funding for area studies began to decline as priorities shifted and the Cold War rationale lost its force. The *Title Ⅳ of Higher Education Act*, a key source of support, faced budget cuts and political attacks, particularly from conservatives who saw area studies as a leftist bastion. At the same time, area studies' position within the university was also changing. The growth of ethnic studies and other interdisciplinary fields presented new competitors for resources and students. Some universities began to question the value of maintaining costly area-specific language and research infrastructure as disciplinary paradigms of globalization and rational choice theory seemed to make deep local knowledge less relevant. Despite these challenges, Area Studies proved resilient and adaptive. Scholars responded to theoretical critiques by developing new frameworks that emphasized cross-regional comparison, transnational connections, and the historical construction of space and scale. Concepts like "globalization" "hybridity", and "diaspora" provided ways to rethink the area studies project for a new era. Institutionally, area studies programs experimented with new organizational forms and funding models. Some centers rebranded themselves around thematic rubrics like "international studies" or "global studies" that cut across traditional area boundaries. Others developed new collaborations with professional schools and emphasized their relevance to global business, health, and environmental issues. The rise of Asian economies and the post-Cold War geopolitical landscape also opened up new rationales and sources of support for area expertise. In the 2000s, events like "9. 11" and the war on terror gave area studies a new prominence, particularly for regions like the Middle East and Central Asia that had previously been relatively neglected. At the same time, the globalization of higher education created new opportunities and challenges, as areas studies programs confronted the need to engage with scholars and institutions from the regions they studied on more equal terms. Today, area studies remains a vital if sometimes embattled part of the academic landscape. Its core commitments to deep linguistic and cultural knowledge, interdisciplinarity, and critical perspectives on power and inequality continue to offer an important counterpoint to more universalizing paradigms in the social sciences and humanities. At the same time, the field continues to grapple with tensions between area-specific and cross-regional approaches, between theoretical and empirical agendas, and between scholarly autonomy and relevance to policy and public debates. Looking forward, the ongoing development of area studies will likely be shaped by a number of trends and challenges. These include the continued rise of non-Western regions as centers of scholarly production and agenda-setting; the blurring of boundaries between domestic and foreign, traditional and modern, and local and global; the growth of new methodologies like digital humanities and data science; and the need to engage with urgent transnational issues like climate change, migration, and global health. As area studies navigates these complexities, it will be important to sustain the field's unique commitment to grounded, contextualized knowledge while also finding new ways to connect that knowledge to broader questions and public concerns. This will require ongoing reflection on the nature and purpose of area expertise, the ethics and politics of cross-cultural representation, and the institutional structures best suited to fostering innovative, interdisciplinary, and globally-engaged scholarship. By grappling with these issues, area studies can continue to offer vital contributions to our understanding of a complex, changing world.

### 1.2.4 Towards an Interdisciplinary, Reflexive, and Engaged Area Studies

Looking forward, area studies scholars are working to bridge disciplinary divides and promote more integrative approaches. This includes efforts to connect humanities and social science perspectives, as well as to engage with emerging theoretical currents and methodologies from fields like cultural studies, postcolonial studies, and science and technology studies. There is also a growing emphasis on reflexivity and positionality in area studies research. Scholars are increasingly attentive to the power dynamics inherent in knowledge production and their own social locations and biases. Collaborative research models that decenter dominant Western paradigms and embrace multiple forms of situated knowledge are gaining traction. In terms of relevance and engagement, area studies scholars are seeking to connect their work to pressing public issues and policy challenges. This includes contributing regional perspectives on global problems like climate change, migration, and public health. Participatory research approaches that involve collaboration with local communities and civil society groups are also becoming more common. Finally, area studies are moving towards a more plural and comparative approach that transcends traditional nation-state and civilizational frames. Scholars are exploring new spatial scales and transregional configurations, from border lands to oceanic basins. Comparative analysis both within and across regions is seen as vital for building theory and identifying broader patterns and processes. The ongoing evolution of area studies will likely be shaped by efforts to globalize and decolonize the field, to bridge scholarly and public engagement, and to harness regional knowledge to address the complex challenges facing an interconnected world. By embracing interdisciplinarity, reflexivity, and ethical collaboration, area studies can offer unique insights into the specificities of place while contributing to larger intellectual and policy conversations. In summary, while area studies continues to grapple with the legacies of its colonial and Cold War origins, the field is undergoing a vibrant transformation in response to new global realities and critical perspectives. Scholars are rethinking inherited assumptions, engaging with emerging issues, and experimenting with innovative research frameworks. The future of area studies will depend on its ability to navigate these challenges and opportunities while remaining grounded in the rigorous study of specific languages, cultures, and histories.

APPLY YOUR KNOWLEDGE

1. How do the legacies of Orientalism and Eurocentrism continue to affect contemporary Area Studies? Discuss the importance of decolonizing knowledge and increasing representation from the Global South.

2. How might the integration of Area Studies and IR contribute to more effective foreign policy decision-making? Provide an example of a current international issue where this integrated approach could be beneficial.

# 1.3 Area Studies in China

The development of Area Studies in China reflects the country's evolving engagement with the world and its growing need for specialized knowledge about different regions. As China's global presence has expanded, so has its investment in understanding the diverse cultures, politics, and economies of various parts of the world. This section traces the historical development of Area Studies in China, examines its current state, and discusses the challenges and future directions of the field.

## 1.3.1 Historical Development

The roots of Area Studies in China can be traced back to the early years of the founding of the People's Republic of China. Even when isolated by the West in the 1950s, China recognized the importance of understanding the outside world. Early international studies in this period focused primarily on the perceived crises in capitalist countries and working-class revolts against capitalism.

The field of Area Studies as we know it today began to take shape in the early 1960s. The discovery of knowing nothing about Africa and Latin America has propelled the establishment of the Institute of Western Asian and African Studies and the Institute of Latin American Studies at the Chinese Academy of Sciences on July 4, 1961. These institutes marked the beginning of systematic area studies research in China, focusing on regions that were seen as potential allies in the developing world.

The development of Area Studies in China can be broadly divided into three waves.

1. The First Wave(1963—1964)

This initial phase saw the establishment of the first dedicated research institutes for Area Studies, focusing primarily on regions of strategic importance to China at the time. In addition to the aforementioned institutes, this period also saw the creation of the Institute of Soviet and East European Studies in 1964, reflecting China's complex relationship with the Soviet Union and Eastern Bloc countries.

2. The Second Wave(1980—1990)

Following China's Reform and Opening Up policy in 1978, there was a renewed emphasis on understanding the world to facilitate China's integration into the global market. This period saw significant growth in Area Studies institutions and programs. The Chinese Academy of Social Sciences(CASS), established in 1977, played a crucial role in this expansion, housing several institutes dedicated to regional studies.

During this period, universities also began to establish their own Area Studies centers. For example, Peking University founded its Institute of Afro-Asian Studies in 1980, which later evolved into the School of International Studies. Similarly, Fudan University established its Center for American Studies in 1985, one of the first of its kind in China.

3. The Third Wave(2000—present)

The most recent phase has been characterized by a more systematic and comprehensive approach to Area Studies, driven largely by government initiatives and the growing recognition of the field's importance for China's global engagement. This period has seen a dramatic increase in the number and diversity of Area Studies programs across China.

## 1.3.2 Institutional Structure and Growth

The institutional landscape of Area Studies in China is diverse, encompassing research institutes, university departments, and government-affiliated think tanks. Key players include:

1. CASS

Established in 1977, CASS houses several institutes dedicated to Area Studies, including the following.

- Institute of Latin American Studies.
- Institute of Russian, Eastern European, and Central Asian Studies.
- Institute of West Asian and African Studies.
- Institute of European Studies.
- Institute of American Studies.
- Institute of Asia-Pacific Studies.

These institutes conduct research, publish academic journals, and provide policy recommendations to the government.

2. Universities

Many of China's top universities have established Area Studies centers. For example,

- Peking University's Institute of Area Studies, founded in 2018, coordinates various regional research centers.
- Fudan University's Center for American Studies, established in 1985, has become one of the leading institutions for the U. S. Studies in China.
- Renmin University's School of International Studies houses several regional research centers, including the Center for European Studies and the Center for African Studies.

3. Provincial Academies

Some provincial academies of social sciences have research institutes focused on neighboring countries or regions. For instance, the Heilongjiang Provincial Academy of Social Sciences has institutes for the study of Russia and Northeast Asia, reflecting the province's geographical proximity to these areas.

4. Ministry of Education Initiative

In 2011, the Ministry of Education launched the "Regional and Country Studies Bases" policy, calling for a nationwide network of Area Studies centers. This initiative has led to the establishment of hundreds of centers across China, with specific requirements for registration and accreditation. By 2018, over 400 research centers had been established at top Chinese universities under this program.

5. Think Tanks

In recent years, China has also seen the rise of think tanks focused on international affairs and regional studies. For example, China Institutes of Contemporary International Relations (CICIR), affiliated with the Ministry of State Security, conducts research on various world regions and provides policy recommendations to the government.

### 1.3.3 Current State and Characteristics

Today, Area Studies in China are characterized by several key features.

1. Interdisciplinary Approach

Chinese Area Studies programs integrate perspectives from various disciplines, including history, political science, economics, anthropology, and cultural studies. This approach allows for a comprehensive understanding of the regions being studied.

2. Policy Orientation

There is a strong emphasis on producing research that can inform policy decisions and support China's global engagement. Many Area Studies centers have direct links to government ministries and provide regular briefings and reports.

3. Language Training

Recognizing the importance of linguistic competence, many Area Studies programs in China include intensive language training components. For example, the Beijing Foreign Studies University offers programs in over 100 foreign languages, many of which are tied to regional studies programs.

4. Comprehensive Coverage

There are now centers and programs dedicated to studying almost every region of the world, reflecting China's global interests. This includes not only traditional areas of focus like East Asia and the United States but also emerging regions of interest such as Africa and Latin America.

5. Rapid Expansion

The number of Area Studies centers has grown dramatically in recent years. According to a report by Ministry of Education, the number of country and regional studies centers increased from just a few dozen in 2011 to over 400 by 2018.

6. Emphasis on Contemporary Issues

While historical understanding is valued, there is a strong focus on contemporary issues and future trends in the regions being studied. This includes topics such as economic development, political transitions, and regional integration processes.

7. Growing International Collaboration

Chinese Area Studies programs are increasingly engaging in international collaborations, including joint research projects, academic exchanges, and co-hosting of conferences with foreign institutions.

## 1.3.4 Challenges and Future Directions

Despite its rapid growth, Area Studies in China face several challenges.

1. Quality Control

The rapid expansion of Area Studies centers has raised concerns about the quality and depth of research produced. There are ongoing efforts to establish evaluation mechanisms and quality standards for these centers.

2. Balancing Theory and Practice

There is an ongoing debate about how to integrate theoretical frameworks with practical, policy-oriented research. Some scholars argue for a more theoretical approach, while others emphasize the need for applied research that can directly inform policy.

3. Language Barriers

Despite increased emphasis on language training, there is still a shortage of experts proficient in less commonly taught languages, particularly for regions like Africa and parts of Southeast Asia.

4. Access to Field Research

Chinese scholars often face difficulties in conducting extended fieldwork in certain regions due to political or logistical constraints. This can limit the depth and nuance of research in some areas.

5. Interdisciplinary Integration

While interdisciplinarity is emphasized, achieving genuine integration of different disciplinary perspectives remains a challenge. Many programs still operate within traditional disciplinary silos.

6. International Collaboration

There is a need for more extensive collaboration with international scholars and institutions to enhance the global perspective of Chinese Area Studies. However, this can be complicated by political sensitivities and differing academic traditions.

7. Addressing Biases

Like Area Studies programs globally, Chinese Area Studies must grapple with potential biases and the legacy of Orientalist approaches to studying other cultures. There is an ongoing need for critical self-reflection within the field.

8. Funding and Resource Allocation

While government support for Area Studies has been substantial, there are concerns about the sustainability of funding, particularly for less strategically important regions.

Looking to the future, several trends are likely to shape the development of Area Studies in China.

1. Increased Focus on Emerging Regions

As China's global interests expand, there is likely to be greater emphasis on studying previously neglected regions, such as parts of Africa and Latin America. This may lead to the establishment of new specialized research centers and programs.

2. Integration of Digital Technologies

The use of big data, digital mapping, and other technological tools is likely to become more prevalent in Area Studies research. This could open up new avenues for analysis and visualization of regional trends.

3. Greater Emphasis on Transnational Issues

As global challenges like climate change and pandemics become more pressing, Area Studies in China may shift towards more transnational and comparative approaches. This could involve more cross-regional studies and a focus on how global issues manifest in different local contexts.

4. Enhanced Policy Relevance

The demand for Area Studies expertise to inform China's foreign policy and global economic engagement is likely to grow. This may lead to closer ties between academic institutions and government agencies, potentially raising questions about academic independence.

5. Diversification of Perspectives

There may be increased efforts to incorporate more diverse viewpoints, including those of scholars from the regions being studied. This could involve more international collaborations and efforts to amplify voices from the Global South.

6. Expansion of Public Diplomacy Role

Area Studies centers may play an increasing role in China's public diplomacy efforts, hosting international conferences, facilitating academic exchanges, and contributing to cultural diplomacy initiatives.

7. Focus on the Belt and Road Initiative

Given the importance of the Belt and Road Initiative (BRI) to China's foreign policy, Area Studies programs are likely to place increased emphasis on countries and regions along the BRI routes.

Area Studies in China have undergone significant development since its inception in the 1960s, reflecting China's changing position in the world and its evolving needs for global knowledge. From its early focus on understanding potential allies in the developing world, it has grown into a comprehensive field covering all regions of the globe. The rapid expansion of Area Studies centers and programs in recent years, driven by government initiatives and growing demand for regional expertise, underscores the field's importance in China's academic and policy landscapes.

However, this growth also brings challenges, including maintaining research quality, balancing theoretical and practical orientations, and addressing potential biases. As China continues to engage more deeply with the world, Area Studies will play a crucial role in informing its global interactions and shaping its understanding of diverse cultures and societies.

The future of Area Studies in China will likely be characterized by greater interdisciplinarity, increased use of digital technologies, and a more nuanced understanding of global complexities. By addressing its current challenges and embracing new approaches, Area Studies in China can contribute significantly to both academic knowledge and practical policy-making, supporting China's role as a major global actor in the 21st century.

As the field continues to evolve, it will be important for Area Studies in China to maintain a balance between serving national interests and contributing to global academic discourse. This may involve fostering more open academic exchanges, encouraging critical perspectives, and engaging more deeply with international scholarly communities. By doing so, Area Studies in China can not only enhance its own development but also contribute to a more diverse and inclusive global academic landscape.

APPLY YOUR KNOWLEDGE

1. Compare and contrast the three waves of Area Studies development in China. How did the focus and approach change over time?

2. Evaluate the role of the CASS in the growth of Area Studies in China. What specific institutes does it house?

3. In light of the increasing use of digital technologies and the need for a more nuanced understanding of global complexities, what new methodologies and approaches should Chinese Area Studies adopt to enhance its relevance and effectiveness in the 21st century?

## AFTER CLASS

### KEY TERMS

| | | |
|---|---|---|
| Area Studies | Global relevance | Digital humanities |
| Hybridity | Transnational approaches | Diaspora |
| Big data analytics | Regional expertise | International Relations |

### EXTENSION

● Exploring Indigenous Knowledge Systems

Indigenous knowledge systems are crucial for understanding the social, cultural, and ecological dynamics of various regions. These knowledge systems encompass the beliefs, practices, and traditions of indigenous peoples, which have been developed over generations. They offer valuable insights into sustainable practices, biodiversity conservation, and community resilience. For instance, the traditional ecological knowledge of indigenous peoples in the Amazon rainforest has been instrumental in preserving biodiversity and managing natural resources sustainably. Recognizing and integrating indigenous perspectives into Area Studies can enhance our understanding of regional complexities and inform more effective policy-making.

## Activity

1. Research Assignment

Students will select an indigenous community from a specific region (e. g. , native American tribes in North America, indigenous groups in the Amazon, or aboriginal communities in Australia) and investigate their knowledge systems, cultural practices, and contributions to sustainable development.

2. Group Presentation

Each student will present their findings, focusing on

(1) the historical context of the indigenous community;

(2) key aspects of their knowledge systems and practices;

(3) the relevance of these systems to contemporary global challenges, such as climate change and biodiversity loss.

3. Reflection

Students will write a short reflection (1 ~ 2 paragraphs) on how integrating indigenous knowledge into Area Studies can enhance our understanding of regional dynamics and inform global policy.

Suggested resources

Local and Indigenous Knowledge Systems (LINKS) | UNESCO (https://www.unesco.org/en/links)

What Does Indigenous Knowledge Mean? A Compilation of Attributes. (https://www.ictinc.ca/blog/what-does-indigenous-knowledge-mean)

● The Impact of Digital Technology on Area Studies

The advent of digital technology has transformed the field of Area Studies, providing new tools for research, collaboration, and dissemination of knowledge. Digital platforms enable scholars to access vast amounts of data, engage with diverse communities, and share their findings with a global audience. For example, digital mapping tools can visualize socio-political dynamics in specific regions, while online databases provide access to historical documents and contemporary reports. The use of social media and online forums also facilitates dialogue between scholars and local communities, enriching the research process and ensuring that diverse voices are heard.

## Activity

1. Exploration of Digital Tools

Students will research various digital tools and platforms that are currently used in Area Studies(e. g. , digital mapping, online databases, social media engagement). They should evaluate how these tools enhance research and collaboration.

2. Discussion

Organize a class discussion on the implications of digital technology for the future of Area Studies. Students should consider questions such as:

(1) How can digital tools improve access to knowledge and foster collaboration?

(2) What challenges do scholars face in integrating digital technology into their research?

(3) How can digital platforms ensure the representation of marginalized voices in Area Studies?

Suggested resources

Area Studies and the Challenges of the Digital Era-Online Discussion (https://europeamerica. de/news-and-events/detail/area-studies-and-the-challenges-of-the-digital-era-online-discussion. html)

CASE STUDY

● The Role of Area Studies in Understanding Climate Change in the Arctic

The Arctic region is one of the most rapidly changing environments on Earth, experiencing significant impacts from climate change. As global temperatures rise, the Arctic is warming at twice the rate of the global average, leading to the melting of ice sheets, rising sea levels, and disruptions to ecosystems that have thrived for millennia. Understanding these changes requires an interdisciplinary approach that incorporates scientific research, indigenous knowledge, and socio-political analysis. Area Studies provides the necessary framework to analyze these complex interactions and their implications for local communities and global systems.

## Key Issues

1. Indigenous Knowledge and Climate Adaptation

Indigenous communities in the Arctic, such as the Inuit in Canada and Alaska, have lived in harmony with their environment for generations. Their traditional ecological knowledge (TEK) offers valuable insights into sustainable practices and adaptation strategies in response to climate change. For example, Inuit hunters have observed changes in animal migration patterns and ice conditions, which are crucial for their hunting practices. By integrating TEK with scientific research, policymakers can develop more effective climate adaptation strategies that respect local traditions and knowledge.

A notable example of this integration is the work done by the Inuit Circumpolar Council (ICC), which emphasizes the importance of incorporating indigenous perspectives into climate policy discussions. The ICC advocates for the rights of Inuit communities and promotes sustainable practices that are informed by TEK.

2. Geopolitical Implications

The melting Arctic ice is opening new shipping routes and access to untapped natural resources, leading to increased geopolitical competition among Arctic nations, including the United States, Russia, Canada, and Norway. Understanding the historical context of territorial claims and the socio-political dynamics among these nations is essential for navigating potential conflicts and fostering cooperation in the region. For instance, the Northern Sea Route and the Northwest Passage are becoming increasingly navigable due to melting ice, prompting countries to assert claims over these routes. This geopolitical competition raises questions about sovereignty, resource management, and environmental protection.

3. Global Climate Impact

Changes in the Arctic have far-reaching implications for global climate patterns. The loss of sea ice affects ocean circulation and weather patterns across the globe, contributing to extreme weather events in other regions. For example, the Arctic's warming has been linked to changes in the jet stream, which can lead to prolonged heatwaves or cold spells in the mid-latitudes.

Area Studies can help analyze how regional changes in the Arctic impact global climate systems and inform international climate agreements. The Arctic Climate Impact Assessment (ACIA) highlights the importance of integrating scientific research with local knowledge to understand these dynamics.

## Examples of Organizations and Initiatives

1. ICC

Represents Inuit communities across Arctic nations and advocates for the protection of their rights and the environment. The ICC emphasizes the importance of incorporating indigenous perspectives into climate policy discussions.

2. Arctic Council

An intergovernmental forum that promotes cooperation among Arctic states on issues related to sustainable development and environmental protection. The Arctic Council's Working Groups, such as the Arctic Monitoring and Assessment Program (AMAP), conduct assessments on climate change impacts in the region.

3. The Arctic Climate Impact Assessment (ACIA)

A comprehensive report that assesses the impacts of climate change in the Arctic, highlighting the importance of integrating scientific research with local knowledge.

## Key Questions

1. How do indigenous communities in the Arctic perceive and respond to climate change, and what role does their traditional ecological knowledge play in adaptation strategies?

2. What are the geopolitical implications of changing Arctic conditions, particularly regarding resource extraction and territorial claims among Arctic nations?

3. How can Area Studies contribute to a more nuanced understanding of the intersection between climate science and local knowledge in the Arctic?

CLASS DISCUSSION

Facilitate a discussion on the importance of interdisciplinary approaches in addressing climate change and the role of Area Studies in informing policy decisions.

FOR FUN

1. Websites to visit

(1) The Harvard Academy for International and Area Studies. Weatherhead Center for International Affairs

(2) Homepage—Association for Asian Studies

2. Movie to see

*The Lives of Others* (2006)

Set in East Germany during the Cold War, this film provides insights into life under the surveillance of the Stasi, the East German secret police

3. Book to read

吴小安,《区域与国别之间》

吴小安,曾任北京大学世界史研究院教授,中国华侨历史学会副会长,现任华侨大学讲席教授兼华侨华人与区域国别研究院创院院长,主要从事东南亚研究、区域国别研究。

# Unit 2 Area Studies: Theory and Method

I never underestimate the power of a theorist to come up with a new model.

—Saul Perlmutter

A method is more important than a discovery, since the right method will lead to new and even more important discoveries.

—Lev Landau

## LEARNING OUTCOMES

■ Compare different theories and approaches and how they contribute to current debates on social science methods, particularly regarding qualitative and mixed-method research.

■ Discuss the growing recognition of the relevance of Area Studies knowledge in understanding the interaction between regional orders and global power structures.

■ Apply Area Studies perspectives to analyze contemporary global challenges, such as climate change, migration, and social inequality.

■ Analyze the potential benefits and risks of extending one's field of vision beyond one's primary area of expertise in area studies.

■ Explore emerging themes and research agendas in Area Studies and assess their implications for the future direction of the field.

## BEFORE CLASS

■ Ariel Ira Ahram, Patrick Köllner and Rudra Sil. *Comparative Area Studies Methodological Rationales and Cross-Regional Applications*. Oxford University Press, 2018

After you read the above materials, please answer the following questions.

1. How does Comparative Area Studies (CAS) balance context-sensitive understandings of diverse locales with cross-regional qualitative research?

2. What are the epistemological, methodological, and practical challenges in

conducting cross-regional comparative research?

3. How can creatively designed contextualized comparisons of cases from different regions generate novel insights into topics like protests, rebellions, anti-corruption campaigns, resource booms, and the organization of production?

4. How does CAS aim to connect scholarly debates taking place within separate area studies communities to each other and to theoretical problems driving social science research?

## 2.1 Major Theoretical Frameworks in Area Studies

Area Studies has been shaped by a range of influential theoretical frameworks that provide lenses for analyzing the complex social, political, economic, and cultural dynamics of different world regions. These frameworks reflect the field's engagement with broader debates in the social sciences and humanities, as well as its efforts to grapple with the legacies of colonialism and the challenges of globalization. In this section, we will explore four key theoretical frameworks that have had a significant impact on Area Studies: modernization theory, dependency theory, world-systems theory, and postcolonial theory.

### 2.1.1 Modernization Theory

Modernization theory, which gained prominence in the 1950s and 1960s, posits that societies progress through similar stages of development, from traditional to modern. It emphasizes the role of internal factors such as education, market-based economy, and democratic political structures in driving economic and social development. A key proponent of modernization theory is Walt Whitman Rostow, an American economist and political theorist. In his influential book *The Stages of Economic Growth: A Non-Communist Manifesto* (1960), Rostow proposed five stages of economic growth: traditional society, preconditions for take-off, take-off, drive to maturity, and age of high mass consumption. He argued that all societies could modernize by following this linear path.

Another influential modernization theorist is Seymour Martin Lipset, a political sociologist. In his article "Some Social Requisites of Democracy: Economic Development and Political Legitimacy" (1959), Lipset argued that economic development, particularly the growth of the middle class, was a key prerequisite for the emergence and sustainability of democratic political systems.

However, critics argue that modernization theory is Eurocentric, assuming that the Western model of development is universally applicable and desirable. It fails to account for the unique historical, cultural, and political contexts of different regions. Scholars like Andre Gunder Frank, a German-American economic historian and sociologist, criticized modernization theory for ignoring the role of colonialism and global power structures in shaping the development trajectories of non-Western societies.

### 2.1.2 Dependency Theory

Dependency theory emerged in the 1960s as a critique of modernization theory. It argues that global inequality is perpetuated by the exploitation of peripheral regions by core countries. Resources flow from poor "periphery" countries to rich "core" countries, enriching the latter at the expense of the former.

Key figures in dependency theory include Andre Gunder Frank, Immanuel Wallerstein, and Samir Amin. Andre Gunder Frank, in his book *Capitalism and Underdevelopment in Latin America* (1967), argued that the development of the core was predicated on the underdevelopment of the periphery. He rejected the notion that underdeveloped areas were merely primitive versions of developed countries, instead emphasizing the structural constraints imposed by the global capitalist system. Immanuel Wallerstein, an American sociologist, developed world-systems theory as an extension of dependency theory. In his seminal work *The Modern World-System I: Capitalist Agriculture and the Origins of the European World-Economy in the Sixteenth Century* (1974), Wallerstein argued that the modern world-system emerged in the 16th century with the expansion of European capitalism. He divided the world into core, semi-periphery, and periphery regions, with unequal power relations and economic exchanges between them. Samir Amin, an Egyptian-French political economist, further developed dependency theory from a Marxist perspective. In his book *Accumulation on a World Scale: A Critique of the Theory of Underdevelopment* (1974), Amin argued that the global capitalist system was characterized by unequal exchange between the core and the periphery, with the latter providing cheap labor and raw materials to fuel the growth of the former.

Dependency theorists can be divided into two main camps: liberal reformists who advocate for targeted policy interventions, and neo-Marxists who propose a more radical restructuring of the global economy, often through socialist revolution. However, both camps emphasize the need to challenge the structural inequalities embedded in the global capitalist system.

## 2.1.3 World-systems Theory

World-systems theory, developed by Immanuel Wallerstein in the 1970s, conceptualizes the global economy as a hierarchical system divided into core, semi-peripheral, and peripheral regions. It emphasizes the interdependence and unequal power relations between different parts of the world. Wallerstein's key works include *The Modern World-System I: Capitalist Agriculture and the Origins of the European World-Economy in the Sixteenth Century* (1974), *The Modern World-System Ⅱ: Mercantilism and the Consolidation of the European World-Economy, 1600—1750* (1980), and *The Modern World-System Ⅲ: The Second Era of Great Expansion of the Capitalist World-Economy, 1730s—1840s* (1989). In these works, Wallerstein traced the emergence and evolution of the modern world-system, arguing that it was characterized by the rise of European capitalism, colonialism, and the division of labor on a global scale. A key concept in world-systems theory is hegemony—the dominance of one state over others in the interstate system. Hegemonic powers, such as the United Kingdom in the 19th century and the United States after World War Ⅱ, play a crucial role in maintaining the stability of the capitalist world-economy. However, Wallerstein argued that hegemony is inherently unstable, with cycles of rise and decline as new challengers emerge. World-systems theory has been influential in various disciplines, including sociology, anthropology, and geography. Scholars like Christopher Chase-Dunn, an American sociologist, have further developed the theory, examining issues such as the rise and fall of hegemonic powers, the role of social movements, and the prospects for a more equitable world order. However, critics argue that world-systems theory is overly deterministic, neglecting the role of human agency and local specificities. Some scholars, like Theda Skocpol, an American sociologist and political scientist, have criticized world-systems theory for its lack of attention to the internal dynamics of states and societies.

## 2.1.4 Postcolonial Theory

Postcolonial theory, which gained traction in the 1980s, examines the cultural, political, and economic legacies of colonialism. It challenges Eurocentric assumptions and power structures, emphasizing the agency and resistance of colonized peoples. Edward Said, a Palestinian-American literary theorist and cultural critic, was a key figure in the development of postcolonial theory. In his influential book *Orientalism* (1978), Said argued that Western representations of the "Orient" were deeply implicated in colonial power structures, creating and perpetuating stereotypes that justified domination. He showed how academic knowledge production about the Middle East and Asia had historically been shaped by colonial interests and biases.

Other prominent postcolonial theorists include Homi Bhabha, an Indian-English scholar, and Gayatri Chakravorty Spivak, an Indian literary theorist and feminist critic. Bhabha, in his book *The Location of Culture* (1994), developed the concepts of hybridity, mimicry, and ambivalence to describe the complex cultural interactions and power dynamics between colonizers and colonized. Spivak, in her essay "*Can the Subaltern Speak?*" (1988), interrogated the ability of marginalized groups, particularly women in the Global South, to have their voices heard and represented in academic and political discourse. Postcolonial theory has had a significant impact on various fields, including literature, cultural studies, history, and anthropology. In Area Studies, postcolonial perspectives have prompted a rethinking of traditional regional boundaries and a greater attention to transnational connections and power dynamics. Scholars have used postcolonial theory to critique the Eurocentrism of earlier Area Studies approaches and to foreground the perspectives and experiences of people in the Global South. However, postcolonial theory has also faced criticism from various quarters. Some scholars argue that it can lead to an essentialization of cultural differences and a romanticization of pre-colonial societies. Others critique postcolonial theory for its focus on cultural and discursive issues at the expense of material and economic factors.

## 2.1.5 Summary

These major theoretical frameworks—modernization theory, dependency theory, world-systems theory, and postcolonial theory—have shaped the evolution of Area Studies, providing lenses for analyzing the complex social, political, economic, and cultural dynamics of different world regions. While each theory has its strengths and limitations, they collectively contribute to a more nuanced and critical understanding of global inequalities, development processes, and power relations. As Area Studies continues to evolve in the 21st century, scholars are increasingly drawing on insights from multiple theoretical frameworks and disciplines to address pressing global challenges. This includes engaging with new theoretical developments, such as decolonial theory, which pushes for a more radical decentering of Western epistemologies and a greater emphasis on the knowledge and experiences of marginalized communities in the Global South. Ultimately, the ongoing dialogue and debate between different theoretical perspectives is crucial for the vitality and relevance of Area Studies. By critically engaging with the assumptions and implications of different frameworks, scholars can generate new insights and approaches for understanding and addressing the complex realities of our interconnected world.

The major theoretical frameworks discussed in this section—modernization theory, dependency theory, world-systems theory, and postcolonial theory—have each contributed to the evolution of Area Studies in significant ways. Modernization theory, despite its limitations and critiques, played a crucial role in shaping early Area Studies programs and research agendas, particularly in the context of the Cold War and decolonization. Dependency theory and world-systems theory, emerging as critiques of modernization theory, pushed Area Studies scholars to grapple more directly with questions of power, inequality, and global economic structures. Postcolonial theory, meanwhile, has prompted a fundamental rethinking of the field's assumptions and methodologies, challenging Eurocentric biases and foregrounding the agency and perspectives of people in the Global South.

As Area Studies continues to evolve in the 21st century, these theoretical frameworks remain important touchstones for scholars seeking to understand the complexities of different world regions. At the same time, the field is also engaging with new theoretical developments, such as decolonial theory and critical race theory, which push for even more radical questioning of Western epistemologies and power structures. Ultimately, the ongoing dialogue and debate between different theoretical perspectives is crucial for the vitality and relevance of Area Studies. By critically engaging with the assumptions and implications of different frameworks, scholars can generate new insights and approaches for understanding and addressing the pressing challenges facing our interconnected world.

APPLY YOUR KNOWLEDGE

1. Compare and contrast modernization theory and dependency theory as frameworks for understanding development processes in different world regions. What are the key assumptions and limitations of each theory, and how have they influenced Area Studies research agendas?

2. Analyze the concept of hegemony in world-systems theory and its relevance for understanding power relations and inequalities in the global economy. How have scholars like Immanuel Wallerstein and Christopher Chase-Dunn developed and applied this concept in their works?

## 2.2 Key Conceptual Approaches in Area Studies

Area Studies employs a range of conceptual approaches to analyze the complex dynamics of different world regions. These approaches reflect the field's interdisciplinary nature and its engagement with diverse methodological traditions. In this section, we will explore four key conceptual approaches: comparative analysis, historical analysis, cultural studies, and political economy.

### 2.2.1 Comparative Analysis

Comparative analysis is a fundamental approach in Area Studies, involving the systematic comparison of different regions, countries, or cases to identify similarities, differences, and broader patterns. By comparing and contrasting, scholars can test theories, generate new insights, and develop a more nuanced understanding of the factors shaping social, political, economic, and cultural realities in different contexts. The comparative approach has a long tradition in the social sciences, with early works like Alexis de Tocqueville's *Democracy in America* (1835) using comparison to analyze political systems. In Area Studies, comparative analysis has been used to study a wide range of issues, from democratization processes to social movements to economic development strategies. One influential example of comparative analysis in Area Studies is Barrington Moore's *Social Origins of Dictatorship and Democracy* (1966). Moore compared the historical trajectories of six countries to identify the social and economic conditions that led to the emergence of democratic, fascist, or communist regimes. His work highlighted the importance of factors such as the strength of the bourgeoisie, the role of the landed elite, and the nature of class coalitions in shaping political outcomes. Another notable example is Theda Skocpol's *States and Social Revolutions* (1979), which compared the French, Russian, and Chinese revolutions to develop a structural theory of social revolutions. Skocpol argued that these revolutions were not simply the result of class struggles, but rather emerged from a combination of international pressures, state crises, and peasant rebellions. Comparative analysis in Area Studies often involves comparing countries or regions that share certain characteristics but differ in others. For example, a study might compare the economic development strategies of East Asian countries like South Korea and Singapore, which achieved rapid industrialization in the late 20th century. By examining the similarities and differences in their approaches, such as the role of the state, trade policies, and investment in education, researchers can identify key factors that contributed to their economic success. Comparative analysis can also be used to study the diffusion of ideas, practices, and institutions across different regions. For instance, scholars have compared the spread of social movements like feminism or environmentalism in different parts of the world, examining how these movements adapt to local contexts and interact with pre-existing cultural and political traditions. In recent years, there has been growing interest in comparative studies of urbanization and urban development across different world regions. For example, the "Global Suburbanism" project, led by Roger Keil at York University, compares suburban development patterns in North America, Europe, Africa, and Asia. By examining the similarities and differences in these patterns, the project aims to develop a more global understanding of suburbanization processes and their social, political, and environmental implications.

However, comparative analysis also faces challenges and limitations. Selecting appropriate cases for comparison requires careful consideration of their comparability and the variables that might affect the outcomes of interest. There is also a risk of oversimplification or overgeneralization when comparing complex and diverse regions. Area Studies scholars must be attentive to the specificities of each context while still identifying meaningful patterns and regularities.

### 2.2.2 Historical Analysis

Historical analysis is another central approach in Area Studies, involving the examination of the past to understand the present. By tracing the historical roots of contemporary issues, scholars can better understand the complex processes and events that have shaped different regions over time. Area Studies has long been influenced by historical approaches, with many early Area Studies programs emerging out of history departments. The field has also been shaped by the rise of social and cultural history in the late 20th century, which emphasized the study of everyday life, popular culture, and marginalized groups. One influential example of historical analysis in Area Studies is Benedict Anderson's *Imagined Communities* (1983). Anderson examined the historical emergence of nationalism in different parts of the world, arguing that nations are socially constructed "imagined communities" rather than natural or primordial entities. His work highlighted the role of print media, vernacular languages, and colonial administrative practices in shaping the development of national identities. Another important work is Eric Wolf's *Europe and the People Without History* (1982), which challenged Eurocentric narratives of world history by examining the complex interactions between European and non-European societies. Wolf argued that these interactions, often characterized by conquest, colonialism, and exploitation, were central to the development of the modern world system. Historical analysis in Area Studies often involves the use of primary sources such as archival documents, oral histories, and material artifacts. By examining these sources, scholars can gain insights into the lived experiences and perspectives of people in different historical contexts. For example, a study of the Indian independence movement might draw on the personal papers and speeches of leaders like Mahatma Gandhi and Jawaharlal Nehru, as well as the oral histories of ordinary people who participated in the struggle. Historical analysis can also shed light on the legacies of colonialism and imperialism in different world regions. Scholars have examined how colonial policies and practices shaped the economic, political, and cultural trajectories of colonizcd societies, and how these legacies continue to influence contemporary realities. For instance, studies of African countries have explored how the arbitrary borders drawn by European powers during the "Scramble for Africa" in the late 19th century have contributed to ongoing conflicts and challenges of nation-building. A notable example of this approach is Frederick Cooper's *Africa Since 1940: The Past of the Present* (2002), which examines the complex political, economic, and social transformations in Africa from the late colonial period to the early 21st century. Cooper argues that understanding these transformations requires a careful analysis of the interplay between African agency, colonial legacies, and global forces. However, historical analysis also faces challenges, particularly in terms of the availability and interpretation of historical sources. Many regions have complex and contested histories, with multiple and sometimes conflicting narratives. Scholars must be attentive to issues of power and representation in historical sources, recognizing that they often reflect the perspectives of dominant groups rather than marginalized voices.

## 2.2.3 Cultural Studies

Cultural studies is an interdisciplinary approach that examines the role of culture in shaping social, political, and economic realities. It encompasses the study of various forms of cultural production and expression, including literature, film, music, art, and media, as well as the analysis of cultural practices, identities, and representations. Cultural studies emerged as a distinct field in the 1960s and 1970s, drawing on a range of theoretical influences including Marxism, feminism, and post-structuralism. It has since become an important approach in Area Studies, particularly in the study of postcolonial and diasporic cultures. One influential example of Cultural Studies in Area Studies is Edward Said's *Orientalism* (1978), which examined Western representations of the Middle East and Asia. Said argued that these representations were not neutral or objective, but rather reflected the power relations and ideological assumptions of Western colonialism. His work highlighted the importance of critically analyzing cultural representations and their political implications. Another important work is Paul Gilroy's *The Black Atlantic: Modernity and Double Consciousness* (1993), which examined the cultural productions and identities of African diasporic communities in Europe, the Americas, and the Caribbean. Gilroy argued that these communities were shaped by a complex interplay of African, European, and American cultural influences, and that their experiences challenged conventional understandings of modernity and national identity.

Cultural studies approaches in Area Studies often involve the close reading and interpretation of cultural texts and practices. For example, a study of contemporary

Chinese cinema might examine how films reflect and shape cultural values, social norms, and political ideologies. Scholars might analyze the narrative structures, visual imagery, and character representations in these films, as well as their production, distribution, and reception contexts. Cultural studies also emphasizes the study of popular culture and everyday life, recognizing that these domains are important sites of cultural meaning—making and contestation. For instance, a study of Japanese youth culture might examine how young people use fashion, music, and social media to construct and express their identities, and how these practices interact with broader social and economic structures. In recent years, there has been growing interest in the study of digital cultures and new media in Area Studies. For example, the "Digital Asia" project, led by Koichi Iwabuchi at Monash University, examined the impact of digital technologies on cultural production, consumption, and exchange in the Asia-Pacific region. The project explores issues such as the role of social media in political activism, the emergence of new forms of cultural expression, and the challenges of digital inequality and censorship. However, Cultural studies approaches have also faced criticisms and challenges. Some scholars argue that the focus on cultural representation and discourse can neglect the material and economic dimensions of social reality. There are also debates about the politics of representation and the role of the researcher in interpreting and speaking for other cultures.

### 2.2.4 Political Economy

Political economy approaches in Area Studies examine the intersection of political and economic processes in shaping regional realities. They focus on issues such as economic development, trade relations, resource distribution, and the role of the state in managing and regulating economic activity. Political Economy has a long tradition in the social sciences, with roots in the works of classical theorists like Adam Smith and Karl Marx. In Area Studies, Political economy approaches have been influenced by a range of theoretical perspectives, including modernization theory, dependency theory, and world-systems theory. One influential example of Political Economy in Area Studies is Chalmers Johnson's *MITI and the Japanese Miracle* (1982), which examined the role of the Japanese state in promoting economic development in the post-World War Ⅱ period. Johnson argued that Japan's Ministry of International Trade and Industry (MITI) played a crucial role in guiding and coordinating industrial policy, contributing to the country's rapid economic growth and technological advancement. Another important work is Hernando de Soto's *The Mystery of Capital* (2000), which examined the informal economies of developing countries and the challenges of property rights and legal recognition. De Soto argued that the lack of formal property rights was a major obstacle to economic development, and that formalizing these rights could unlock vast amounts of "dead capital" and stimulate entrepreneurship and investment. Political economy approaches in Area Studies often involve the analysis of economic data and indicators, such as GDP growth rates, trade balances, and income inequality measures. Scholars might examine how different economic policies and institutions, such as trade liberalization or state-owned enterprises, affect economic performance, and social welfare in different regions. Political Economy also emphasizes the study of power relations and inequality in shaping economic outcomes. For example, a study of land reform in Latin America might examine how the concentration of land ownership among elite groups has contributed to poverty and social exclusion, and how different political movements and policies have sought to address these inequalities. In recent years, there has been growing interest in the political economy of climate change and environmental sustainability in Area Studies. For example, the "Political Economy of Climate Change in Southeast Asia" project, led by Stathis Kalyvas at Yale University, examines how different countries in the region are responding to the challenges of climate change, and how these responses are shaped by political and economic factors such as energy policies, industrial interests, and social movements. However, Political economy approaches also face challenges and limitations. Economic data and indicators can be incomplete or unreliable, particularly in developing countries with limited statistical capacities. There are also debates about the appropriate balance between state intervention and market forces in promoting economic development, and about the trade-offs between economic growth and other social and environmental goals.

### 2.2.5 Summary

The key conceptual approaches discussed in this section—comparative analysis, historical analysis, cultural studies, and political economy—highlight the diverse and interdisciplinary nature of Area Studies. Each approach offers valuable tools and perspectives for understanding the complex realities of different world regions, from the macro-level analysis of political and economic structures to the micro-level study of cultural practices and everyday life. At the same time, these approaches also face common challenges, such as the need to balance context-specific knowledge with broader theoretical insights, the difficulties of working with limited or biased data sources, and the ethical and political implications of representing and speaking for other cultures and societies.

As Area Studies continues to evolve in the 21st century, scholars are increasingly combining and integrating these different conceptual approaches to develop more holistic and nuanced understandings of regional dynamics. For example, studies of globalization and transnationalism often draw on a combination of comparative, historical, cultural, and political economy perspectives to examine how global processes are reshaping local realities in different parts of the world. Moreover, there is growing recognition of the need to decolonize and diversify Area Studies knowledge production, by centering the voices, experiences, and epistemologies of scholars and communities from the Global South. This involves not only critically examining the Western biases and assumptions embedded in traditional Area Studies approaches, but also actively collaborating with and learning from local scholars and knowledge systems. Ultimately, the vitality and relevance of Area Studies in the 21st century will depend on its ability to embrace and navigate the tensions and possibilities of its interdisciplinary and cross-cultural nature. By combining rigorous empirical analysis with critical theoretical reflection, and by fostering dialogue and collaboration across disciplinary and geographic boundaries, Area Studies scholars can continue to generate valuable insights into the complex and changing realities of our interconnected world.

APPLY YOUR KNOWLEDGE

1. How can comparative analysis help scholars identify the key factors that contribute to economic success in different regions, and what are the potential risks and limitations of this approach?

2. How can the integration of Cultural Studies and Political Economy approaches enhance our understanding of the interplay between cultural practices, economic policies, and power relations in shaping regional dynamics, and what are the potential benefits and drawbacks of such interdisciplinary research?

## 2.3 Theory-Practice Integration in Area Studies

In the 21st century, Area Studies faces the crucial challenge and opportunity of integrating theory and practice to generate knowledge that is both academically rigorous and socially relevant. Scholars in the field are increasingly focused on bridging the gap between theoretical insights and real-world applications, addressing complex global issues through collaborative and interdisciplinary research.

One notable trend is the growing emphasis on partnerships between Area Studies scholars and colleagues from diverse fields such as environmental science, public health, and urban planning. These collaborations allow for a multifaceted approach to pressing challenges that require insights from various perspectives and skill sets. For instance, the University of Michigan's Center for Southeast Asian Studies has initiated a project on sustainable urbanization in Southeast Asia, bringing together experts from architecture, urban planning, and social sciences to investigate the social and environmental consequences of rapid urban growth in the region.

Moreover, Area Studies scholars are increasingly engaging with stakeholders beyond academia, including policymakers, civil society organizations, and local communities. This engagement takes various forms, from providing expert advice and policy recommendations to collaborating on community-based research and action projects. As an example, the University of California, Berkeley's Center for Southeast Asia Studies has collaborated with local organizations in Indonesia to examine the impact of palm oil plantations on indigenous communities and to develop strategies for sustainable land management.

Collaborative research in Area Studies also extends to cross-regional and global issues. The China-Africa Knowledge Project at the Social Science Research Council exemplifies this trend, bringing together scholars from China, Africa, and the United States to explore the social, economic, and political dimensions of China-Africa relations. Through workshops, conferences, and publications, the project aims to generate new knowledge and policy insights on this significant global relationship.

Interdisciplinary collaboration is particularly crucial for addressing complex challenges that transcend traditional area studies boundaries. The study of migration in the Mediterranean region, for instance, requires insights from scholars of Europe, the Middle East, and North Africa, as well as expertise in fields like demography, political science, and anthropology. The Mediterranean Migration Research Group at the European University Institute brings together scholars from multiple disciplines and regions to study this issue, focusing on the drivers, experiences, and governance of migration in the region.

Innovative research methods and technologies are another key aspect of integrating theory and practice in Area Studies. Scholars are increasingly leveraging tools such as geographic information system (GIS), social media analysis, and digital archives to gather and analyze data in novel ways. For example, researchers from the University of Washington and the University of British Columbia used satellite imagery and GIS to map the expansion of oil palm plantations in Indonesia, revealing the extent of deforestation and the role of corporate actors in driving land-use change.

Digital humanities approaches are also opening up new possibilities for Area Studies research, enabling scholars to analyze vast amounts of textual and visual data and to visualize patterns and connections in innovative ways. The Mapping the Republic of Letters project at Stanford University, for instance, uses digital tools to analyze the correspondence networks of Enlightenment-era intellectuals, revealing the global circulation of ideas and the role of key hubs like Paris and London.

The integration of digital tools and methods is also transforming the way Area Studies research is disseminated and engaged with by broader publics. The Torn Apart/Separados project, led by researchers at Columbia University, uses data visualization to map the landscape of immigration detention in the United States. By making this information accessible and interactive, the project aims to inform public debate and policy discussions around immigration issues.

Integrating theory and practice in Area Studies also requires rethinking traditional research outputs and audiences. While academic publications remain important, scholars are increasingly experimenting with new forms of dissemination and engagement, such as policy briefs, multimedia exhibits, and community workshops. For example, the pathways of Vietnamese American Experiences project at the University of California, Irvine, includes a traveling exhibit and a digital archive that showcase the diverse experiences of Vietnamese Americans, making this history accessible to a broad public audience.

Engaged scholarship, which involves collaborating with communities and organizations to co-produce knowledge and drive social change, is another important way that Area Studies researchers are integrating theory and practice. The "Detroit Asian Youth" Project at the University of Michigan, for instance, works with local Asian American youth to document their experiences and perspectives through participatory research methods like photovoice and oral history. The project aims to empower youth as knowledge producers and to use research to advocate for more inclusive and equitable policies and programs.

Finally, integrating theory and practice in Area Studies requires critical reflection on the ethics and politics of knowledge production. As scholars increasingly work across borders and engage with diverse communities, they must grapple with questions of power, representation, and accountability. This includes examining their own positionality as researchers, being transparent about their methods and assumptions, and ensuring that their work benefits the communities they study.

The "Decolonizing Southeast Asian Studies" project at the University of California, Riverside, exemplifies this critical approach, bringing together scholars from Southeast Asia and the diaspora to interrogate the colonial legacies of Area Studies and to develop new frameworks for understanding the region that center local knowledge and perspectives.

Ethical considerations are also crucial when it comes to the use of new research technologies and methods. The use of social media data in Area Studies research, for example, raises important questions about privacy, consent, and the potential for harm. Scholars must develop robust ethical protocols and engage in ongoing reflection and dialogue to ensure that their research practices are responsible and accountable. In conclusion, integrating theory and practice is an ongoing challenge and opportunity for Area Studies in the 21st century. By embracing collaborative and interdisciplinary research, leveraging new methods and technologies, experimenting with innovative forms of dissemination and engagement, and critically reflecting on the ethics and politics of knowledge production, Area Studies scholars can generate insights that are both academically rigorous and socially relevant. As the field continues to evolve, this integration will be crucial for addressing the complex challenges facing our interconnected world and for realizing the transformative potential of Area Studies research.

APPLY YOUR KNOWLEDGE

1. How can partnerships between Area Studies scholars and experts from diverse fields such as environmental science, public health, and urban planning enhance the understanding and addressing of complex global issues, and what are the potential challenges of such interdisciplinary collaborations?

2. How can Area Studies scholars critically reflect on the ethics and politics of knowledge production, particularly in the context of decolonizing research practices and using new technologies like social media analysis?

## 2.4 Contemporary Trends and Future Directions in Area Studies

As Area Studies evolves to address contemporary global challenges, scholars are increasingly embracing innovative methodologies and fostering interdisciplinary collaboration. These approaches are transforming the field, enabling researchers to gain deeper insights into regional issues while also contributing to broader theoretical discussions across disciplines.

1. Integrating Digital Humanities Approaches

Using digital tools for data analysis, visualization, and research dissemination.

The digital humanities have opened up new avenues for research in Area Studies. Scholars are leveraging digital tools to analyze vast amounts of textual and visual data, create interactive maps and visualizations, and disseminate their findings to wider audiences.

For example, the "Mapping the Republic of Letters" project at Stanford University uses digital tools to analyze correspondence networks of Enlightenment-era intellectuals across Europe and the Americas. This approach has revealed previously hidden patterns of intellectual exchange and influence, challenging traditional narratives about the flow of ideas during this period.

Similarly, the "Digital Silk Road" project, a collaboration between Chinese and international scholars, uses GIS to map historical trade routes and cultural exchanges along the Silk Road. This digital approach allows researchers to visualize complex spatial and temporal data, providing new insights into the economic and cultural connections that shaped Eurasian history.

2. Employing Big Data Analytics

Leveraging large datasets for new insights into regional and global patterns.

The availability of large datasets and advanced analytical tools has enabled Area Studies scholars to identify patterns and trends that were previously difficult to discern. This approach is particularly valuable for understanding complex regional dynamics and their global implications.

For instance, researchers studying political behavior in Southeast Asia have used social media data to analyze public opinion trends and political mobilization patterns. By applying natural language processing and sentiment analysis to millions of social media posts, scholars can track the spread of political ideas and the formation of online communities across national borders.

In African Studies, big data analytics have been employed to study climate change impacts and adaptation strategies. Researchers have combined satellite imagery, weather station data, and agricultural surveys to create predictive models of crop yields and food security risks across different regions of the continent. This data-driven approach allows for more targeted interventions and policy recommendations.

3. Fostering Interdisciplinary Collaboration

Bringing together scholars from diverse fields to address complex regional issues.

The complex nature of contemporary global challenges requires expertise from multiple disciplines. Area Studies programs are increasingly fostering collaborations between scholars from diverse fields to address multifaceted regional issues.

One example is the "Urban Sustainability in the Arctic" project, which brings together climatologists, urban planners, anthropologists, and indigenous studies scholars to examine the unique challenges faced by Arctic cities. This interdisciplinary approach allows for a holistic understanding of how climate change, urbanization, and cultural factors intersect in this rapidly changing region.

Another instance is the "Global Health Security in Southeast Asia" initiative, which combines expertise from epidemiologists, political scientists, and anthropologists to study pandemic preparedness and response in the region. This collaborative effort has produced insights into how cultural practices, governance structures, and health systems interact to shape regional health outcomes.

4. Developing Comparative and Collaborative Research

Creating opportunities for scholars working on different regions to identify broader patterns and processes.

Comparative research across regions can reveal broader patterns and processes that might not be apparent when studying a single area in isolation. Area Studies programs are increasingly creating opportunities for scholars to engage in cross-regional comparisons and collaborations.

The "Authoritarianism in the Global South" project, for example, brings together scholars studying authoritarian regimes in Latin America, Africa, and Asia. By comparing case studies from different regions, researchers have identified common patterns in how authoritarian leaders maintain power, as well as unique regional factors that influence regime stability and change.

Similarly, the "Comparative Postcolonial Urban Studies" network connects scholars studying cities in former colonies across Africa, Asia, and the Caribbean. This collaborative approach has yielded new insights into how colonial legacies continue to shape urban development and social inequalities in diverse postcolonial contexts.

5. Engaging in Participatory and Community-based Research Methods

Collaborating with local communities in knowledge production.

Area Studies scholars are increasingly recognizing the importance of engaging with local communities in the research process. Participatory and community-based research methods not only produce more nuanced and contextually grounded knowledge but also help to address power imbalances in academic knowledge production.

For instance, the "Indigenous Knowledge and Climate Change Adaptation" project in the Pacific Islands involves local communities as co-researchers in documenting traditional ecological knowledge and developing climate adaptation strategies. This approach ensures that indigenous perspectives are central to the research process and outcomes.

In Latin American Studies, scholars have employed participatory action research methods to study social movements and grassroots organizations. By collaborating closely with community activists, researchers gain deeper insights into local political dynamics while also contributing to the goals of the movements they study.

These methodological innovations and interdisciplinary collaborations are reshaping

Area Studies, making the field more dynamic and responsive to contemporary global challenges. By integrating digital tools, leveraging big data, fostering interdisciplinary collaboration, developing comparative approaches, and engaging with local communities, Area Studies scholars are producing more nuanced and impactful research.

However, these new approaches also present challenges, including the need for new skills and training, ethical considerations in data collection and community engagement, and the potential for technological disparities to reinforce existing power imbalances in knowledge production. As Area Studies continues to evolve, addressing these challenges while harnessing the potential of new methodologies will be crucial for the field's future relevance and impact.

APPLY YOUR KNOWLEDGE

1. How are Area Studies scholars balancing the need for deep regional expertise with the demand for addressing broader global issues? Discuss the challenges and opportunities this presents.

2. How are new methodologies like digital humanities and big data analytics transforming Area Studies research? What are some potential pitfalls and ethical considerations that scholars should keep in mind when adopting these approaches?

## AFTER CLASS

### KEY TERMS

| | |
|---|---|
| Interdisciplinary Approaches | Decolonization |
| Comparative Analysis | Globalization |
| Historical Context | Transnationalism |
| Cultural Studies | Postcolonial Theory |
| Political Economy | Empirical Research |

### EXTENSION

● Field Study Opportunities in Area Studies

Field study is an essential component of Area Studies, providing students with the opportunity to engage directly with the regions they study. These immersive experiences allow for the application of theoretical knowledge in real-world contexts, enhancing understanding of local cultures, societies, and environments. Field study programs often incorporate interdisciplinary approaches, drawing from various academic disciplines to address complex regional issues. For instance, the Center for Southeast Asian Studies at the University of Michigan offers field study opportunities that combine insights from anthropology, political science, and environmental studies to explore pressing issues in the region, such as climate change and cultural preservation.

## Examples of Field Study Programs

1. Rollins College Field Study Programs

Rollins College offers a variety of field study programs that emphasize hands-on experiences and active engagement with local experts. These programs provide students with immersive learning opportunities in diverse locations, such as winter field studies in France, spring break field studies in Cambodia, and summer programs in Costa Rica focused on environmental studies. Each program typically lasts from one to three weeks, allowing students to earn academic credit while exploring the cultural and historical contexts of the regions they visit.

2. Community Studies Program at UC Santa Cruz

The Community Studies Program at UC Santa Cruz incorporates a full-time field study component, allowing students to engage with organizations working for social change. Students choose placements related to health justice and economic justice, working with community health clinics, immigrant rights centers, and various advocacy organizations. Possible locations for these placements include urban centers like San Francisco, New York City, and even international opportunities in Guatemala. This program emphasizes experiential education and the importance of understanding local contexts in addressing social issues.

3. The School for Field Studies (SFS)

The School for Field Studies offers immersive study abroad programs that combine academic coursework with hands-on field research in various countries. Programs focus on environmental studies, wildlife conservation, and sustainable development, providing students with the opportunity to conduct research in diverse ecosystems, such as the Amazon rainforest or the coastal regions of East Africa. Students engage with local communities and contribute to ongoing research projects, gaining valuable insights into the ecological and cultural dynamics of the regions they study.

## Activity

Engaging with Field Study in Area Studies

1. Research Assignment

Select a specific field study program or project related to Area Studies (e. g. , a summer field school in Southeast Asia, an internship with an NGO in Latin America, or a research project in Sub-Saharan Africa) and investigate its objectives, methodologies, and outcomes. Then, analyze how the program integrates interdisciplinary perspectives and contributes to a deeper understanding of the region.

2. Field Study Reflection

After participating in a field study experience or reviewing a selected program, you can write a reflective essay (2 ~ 3 pages) for discussing.

(1) The key learnings and insights gained from the field study experience.

(2) How the experience challenged or reinforced their understanding of the region?

(3) The importance of field study in bridging the gap between theoretical knowledge and practical application in Area Studies.

3. Group Discussion

Organize a class discussion on the significance of field study in Area Studies. You should consider questions such as adove following.

(1) How does field study enhance the understanding of cultural and social dynamics in a region?

(2) What are the ethical considerations when conducting field research in diverse communities?

(3) In what ways can field study experiences inform policy-making and community engagement?

Suggested Resources

"The School for Field Studies" (https://www.fieldstudies.org)

CASE STUDY

● The Political Economy of Development in Southeast Asia

The countries of Southeast Asia have experienced widely varying trajectories of economic development over the past several decades. While some, like Singapore and Malaysia, have achieved high levels of per capita income and industrialization, others like Myanmar and Cambodia remain relatively poor and agrarian. A key factor in explaining these divergent outcomes is the role of politics and the state in shaping economic policies and institutions.

1. The Developmental State Model

Several Southeast Asian countries, notably Singapore, Malaysia, Thailand, and Indonesia, pursued a "developmental state" model of economic growth in the post-independence period. This approach involved above following.

(1) An activist, interventionist role for the state in guiding and coordinating economic development.

(2) Close ties between the state and private business, with the state providing incentives and protection to favored industries.

(3) Emphasis on export-oriented industrialization and integration into global supply chains.

(4) Investments in human capital development through education and training.

In Singapore, the state played a leading role in economic planning and investment through state-owned enterprises and sovereign wealth funds. Malaysia pursued a similar model of state-led development, with the state also using affirmative action policies like the New Economic Policy to promote Malay business interests.

Thailand and Indonesia relied more on private enterprise, but the state still played a key role in providing infrastructure, credit, and protection to strategic industries. The "technocratic" economic teams in these countries, often educated in the West, were given significant autonomy to formulate and implement economic policies.

2. The Role of Political Stability

A common thread across the high-performing Southeast Asian economies was an extended period of political stability that enabled the state to pursue long-term development strategies. Singapore and Malaysia have been dominated by single ruling parties for decades. Thailand despite periodic military coups, has maintained a basic continuity of economic policies. Indonesia under Suharto's New Order regime (1966—1998) provided a stable environment for investment and growth.

In contrast, countries like the Philippines, Myanmar, and Cambodia have experienced more political instability, frequent changes in leadership, and a more adversarial relationship between the state and private sector. The Philippinesin particular has been characterized by a "cacique democracy" where political power is concentrated in the hands of a few elite families. This has made it difficult to implement consistent, long-term economic policies.

3. The Developmental State in Crisis

The developmental state model came under strain in 1990s with the Asian Financial Crisis. Countries that had relied heavily on foreign capital inflows and short-term borrowing were hit hard by the crisis. The IMF-led bailouts and structural adjustment programs that followed pushed these countries to liberalize their economies and reduce the state's role in directing investment.

The crisis revealed the vulnerabilities of the developmental state model, including cronyism, corruption, and the risks of over-reliance on exports. It also highlighted the need for greater transparency, corporate governance, and financial regulation. In the post-crisis period, Southeast Asian states have had to adapt their development strategies to a more globalized, market-oriented environment.

4. The Persistence of State Capitalism

However, the retreat of the state from the economy has been limited. Many Southeast Asian countries continue to have significant state involvement in strategic industries through state-owned enterprises, sovereign wealth funds, and state-linked companies. The state also remains an important source of infrastructure investment and industrial policy support.

Malaysia under Prime Minister Mahathir Mohamad pursued a "Look East" policy of emulating Japan and South Korea's state-led development model. Indonesia under President Joko Widodo has emphasized infrastructure development and support for domestic industries. Thailand has used policies like the Eastern Economic Corridor to promote high-tech industries.

So while the developmental state model has evolved, the state continues to play a central role in shaping economic outcomes in Southeast Asia. The specific forms of state intervention may have changed, but the idea of the state as a driver of economic transformation remains deeply embedded in the region's political cultures.

5. Implications for Inequality and Sustainability

The developmental state model has delivered rapid economic growth, but it has also generated significant social and environmental costs. Income inequality has risen sharply in many Southeast Asian countries as the benefits of growth have accrued disproportionately to urban elites and foreign investors.

Cronyism and corruption have also undermined the legitimacy of state-business relations. The Philippines under President has pursued a populist, anti-elite agenda in response to these grievances. Indonesia has also seen growing popular protests against inequality and environmental destruction from extractive industries.

So while the developmental state has been a key driver of Southeast Asia's economic success, it now faces challenges in terms of distributional equity, political legitimacy, and environmental sustainability. Navigating these challenges will require rethinking the role of the state in the economy and society. Balancing growth, equity, and sustainability will be a key test for Southeast Asian policymakers in the coming decades.

CLASS DISCUSSION

How have the varying trajectories of economic development in Southeast Asia been influenced by the role of the state, political stability, and the developmental state model, and what challenges do these countries face in balancing growth, equity, and sustainability in the future?

FOR FUN

1. Websites to visit

(1) Latin American Studies Association (LASA)

(2) African Studies Association Portal-ASA

2. Movie to see

*The Namesake* (2006)

Based on JhumpaLahiri's novel, explores themes of immigration and cultural identity relevant to South Asian studies.

3. Book to read

Edward Wadie Said, *Out of Place: A Memoir*

Edward Wadie Said, a Palestinian-American philosopher, academic, literary critic, and political activist. As a professor of literature at Columbia University, he was among the founders of post-colonial studies.

# Unit 3 Regions as Context: Cases from Russia

Russia is a riddle wrapped in a mystery inside an enigma.

—Winston Churchill

Rule 1 on page 1 of the book of war is, "Do not march on Moscow". Various people have tried it, Napoleon and Hitler, and it is no good.

—Bernard Montgomery

## LEARNING OUTCOMES

■ Explain the basic characteristics of Russian geography, including its diverse topography, varied climate zones, and extensive natural resources.

■ Identify the diversity of Russian writers, philosophers, and musicians that have significantly shaped European literature, thought, and art.

■ State the features of Russian political system and its changing complexity.

■ Describe the structure of Russian economy and its position in the world.

■ Summarize the foreign relations of Russia and describe how Russian foreign policies impact global affairs.

## BEFORE CLASS

■ Resource 1 Russian National Character(globalaffairs. ru)

■ Resource 2 Trying to understand the mysterious Russian soul: 10 quotes by famous people about Russia-Russia Beyond(rbth. com)

■ Resource 3 "To suffer is to suffer": Analyzing the Russian national character—Association for Psychological Science(APS)

After you read the above materials, please answer the following questions.

1. How do you summarize the national character of Russia?

2. In terms of national character, are there anything similar between Chinese and Russians?

3. What are the stereotypes towards Russians?

4. How do you think these characters and stereotypes are formed?

# 3.1 Land & People

## 3.1.1 Geography

Russia's expansive territory extends across the eastern part of Europe and the northern part of Asia, making up a large portion of Eurasia. It has the world's fourth-longest coastline, spanning over 37,000 kilometers. Positioned between latitudes 41° and 82° N, and longitudes 19° E and 169° W, Russia stretches approximately 9,000 kilometers from east to west and varies from 2,500 to 4,500 kilometers in width from north to south.

Russia has several major mountain ranges, mostly in its southern parts. The Caucasus Mountains are especially notable, as they include Mount Elbrus, the tallest peak in both Russia and Europe. Other important ranges are the Altai and Sayan Mountains in Siberia, and the East Siberian Mountains and Kamchatka Peninsula in the Russian Far East. Klyuchevskaya Sopka is the highest active volcano not only in Kamchatka but also throughout Russia. The Ural Mountains, which stretch from the north to the south in western Russia, are known for their abundant mineral resources and traditionally mark the divide between Europe and Asia. The country's lowest point is at the Caspian Depression near the Caspian Sea, reaching 28 meters below sea level, which is also the lowest point in continental Europe.

Russia is one of only three countries in the world that border three oceans, and it has coasts along many seas. It has several major islands and groups of islands, like Novaya Zemlya, Franz Josef Land, and Severnaya Zemlya, as well as the New Siberian Islands, Wrangel Island, and the Kuril Islands. Four of the Kuril Islands are the subject of a dispute with Japan, and Sakhalin Island is also significant. The Diomede Islands, which Russia and the United States manage together, are very close to each other, only 3.8 kilometers apart. Kunashir Island, part of the Kuril Islands, is just 20 kilometers from Hokkaido, Japan.

With more than 100,000 rivers, Russia is rich in surface water resources. Its lakes hold about a quarter of the world's unfrozen fresh water. Lake Baikal is especially noteworthy as the deepest lake globally, and it is also the largest freshwater lake by volume. It's holds more than a fifth of the world's fresh surface water. Lakes Ladoga and Onega in the northwest are among Europe's largest lakes. In terms of renewable water resources, Russia is second only to Brazil. The Volga River, seen as Russia's national river, is the longest in Europe and leads to the continent's largest river delta. Siberian rivers like the Ob, Yenisey, Lena, and Amur are among the longest in the world.

## 3.1.2 Climate and Ecosystem

Russia's enormous size and many inland areas being far from the sea result in a predominanty humid continental climate, except in the tundra and the southwest most regions near the Black sea. In the south and east, mountain ranges block warm air from the Indian and Pacific oceans, while the west and north—particularly the European Plain—are open to influences from the Atlantic and Arctic oceans. Much of northwest Russia and central/eastern Siberia generally have a subarctic climate. The inner parts of northeast Siberia, particulary Sakha Republic, experience extremely winters and hosts the Northern Hemisphere's "Pole of Cold", with temperatures as low as −67.8 ℃. However, western parts of northwest Russia and experienc milder winters due to Atlantic-ufluences.

The long Arctic Ocean coastline and Russian Arctic islands have a polar climate. In contrast, the Black Sea's coastal area in Krasnodar Krai, including Sochi, and some North Caucasus regions have a humid subtropical climate with mild, wet winters. East Siberia and the Russian Far East have drier winters than summers, while other parts see more balanced precipitation throughout the year. In most areas, winter precipitation falls as snow. Kaliningrad Oblast's western parts and some southern areas of Krasnodar Krai and the North Caucasus have an oceanic climate. The Lower Volga, Caspian Sea coast, and some southern Siberian areas have a semi-arid climate.

Russia typically experiences two main seasons: winter and summer, with short spring and autumn periods. January (or February along the coast) is the coldest month, and July is usually the hottest. There are significant temperature variations, with colder winters as you move south to north and west to east, and summers can be very hot, even in Siberia. Climate change is leading to more wildfires and thawing permafrost in Russia.

The country's diverse ecosystems range from polar deserts totundras, forest tundras, taigas, various forests, steppes, semi-deserts, and subtropical areas. About half of Russia is forested, making it the world's largest forest area, crucial for absorbing significant amounts of carbon dioxide.

Russia boasts a remarkable range of biodiversity, including thousands of species of vascular plants, bryophytes, lichens, algae, and fungi. Its animal life is equally diverse, with hundreds of mammal species, a large number of bird species, numerous reptiles and amphibians, a significant variety of freshwater and saltwater fish, and an impressive array of invertebrates, many of which are unique to the region. *The Russian Red Data Book*, which lists rare and endangered species, includes over a thousand plant and animal species.

In terms of environmental conservation, Russia has established a substantial number of protected natural areas, which account for a significant portion of the country's total land area. These include dozens of biosphere reserves, national parks, and nature reserves. Russia's efforts in maintaining its forests, especially in the northern taiga and Siberian subarctic tundra, are notable. In recent years, Russia ranked highly on a global index measuring the integrity of forest landscapes, indicating its success in preserving these vital ecosystems.

## 3.1.3 Natural Resources

Russia is home to the world's largest reserves of mineral resources, but many of these are in hard-to-reach areas with extreme weather, making mining costly. The country is particularly rich in mineral fuels, potentially holding up to half of the global coal reserves and substantial petroleum reserves. Coal is found all over Russia, with the biggest deposits in central and eastern Siberia. The main oil fields are in western Siberia and the Volga-Urals region. Russia also possesses about 40% of the world's natural gas reserves, found in places like Siberia's Arctic coast, the North Caucasus, and northwest Russia.

Significant iron ore reserves are near Moscow and along the Ukrainian border in an area known as the Kursk Magnetic Anomaly, where the vast amount of iron ore even affects the Earth's magnetic field. Smaller iron ore deposits are also found in other regions. The Ural Mountains contain smaller quantities of manganese, nickel, tungsten, cobalt, molybdenum, and other elements used in making steel.

Russia also has a wealth of nonferrous metals. Aluminium ore is not as common and is mainly found in the Urals, northwestern Russia, and central Siberia. Copper is more plentiful, with major reserves in the Urals, the Norilsk area in eastern Siberia, and the Kola Peninsula. A large copper deposit in eastern Siberia began to be tapped after the completion of the Baikal-Amur Mainline railroad in 1989.

The North Caucasus, far eastern Russia, and the southern part of the Kuznetsk Basin in Siberia are rich in lead and zinc, often found with copper, gold, silver, and other rare metals. Russia has one of the biggest gold reserves globally, mainly in Siberia and the Urals. Mercury is also found in the central and southern Urals and south-central Siberia.

In terms of other natural resources, the Kama River area in the western Urals has significant potassium and magnesium salt deposits. One of the world's largest apatite deposits is in the central Kola Peninsula. The southwestern Urals and the area southwest of Lake Baikal have rock salt, and there are surface salt deposits in the lower Volga Valley's salt lakes. Sulfur is present in the Urals and the middle Volga Valley.

As for land use, 8% of Russia's land is for arable farming, 4% for permanent pastures, while forests and woodlands cover 46%, and the rest 42% is used for various other purposes.

Furthermore, Russia ranks 33rd in the world for tidal flat areas, with around 1,002 square kilometers of tidal flats, as per a recent global analysis.

### 3.1.4 Population

Russia stands out as one of the world's least densely populated and highly urbanized nations, with the majority of its population concentrated in the western part. The 2021 census, excluding Crimea and Sevastopol, recorded a population of 144.7 million, making Russia the most populous country in Europe and the ninth in the world. The population density is relatively low of 8 inhabitants per square kilometer.

Since the 1990s, Russia has faced a demographic challenge, with the death rate surpassing the birth rate. In 2022, the total fertility rate was estimated at 1.42 children per woman, one of the lowest globally. This has contributed to an aging population, with a median age of 40.3 years. Although Russia saw population growth from 2009 onwards due to reduced death rates, increased birth rates, and immigration, the trend reversed in 2020.

Russia is a diverse, multinational state with over 193 ethnic groups. The 2010 census reported that approximately 81% of the population identified as ethnic Russians, while the remaining 19% represented various ethnic minorities. The majority, which is of European descent (particularly Slavs) forms over four-fifths of Russia's demographic makeup. According to the United Nations, Russia has the world's third-largest immigrant population, approximately 11.6 million, particularly Central Asia.

## 3.1.5 Language

Russian serves as the official and predominant language in Russia. It holds the distinction of being most widely spoken native language in Europe, the most geographically widespread language in Eurasia, and the most spoken Slavic language globally. Russian is officially recognized as one of the two languages aboard the International Space Station and ranks among the six official languages of the United Nations.

Despite the prevalence of Russian, Russia is a multilingual nation, where approximately 100 ~ 150 minority languages are spoken. According to the Russian Census of 2023, 142 million people spoke Russian, while Tatar and Ukrainian were spoken by 5.4 million and 1.7 million individuals, respectively. The constitution permits federal republics within the country the right to designate co-offical languages alongside Russian. Furthermore, it ensures citizens' rights to preserve their native languages and facilitates conditions for their study and development.

## 3.1.6 Culture

Russian writers and philosophers have significantly shaped European literature and thought, contributing to the broader intellectual landscape. The influence of Russians extends beyond literature to various domains, including classical music, ballet, sports, painting, cinema. Russia's impact is evident in cultural, artistic, and scientific spheres, with notable contributions to space exploration and technology.

The country boasts 31 UNESCO World Heritage Sites, 24 of which are cultural treasures, with a further 27 sites on the tentative list. The extensive Russian diaspora has played a crucial role in disseminating Russian culture worldwide. Symbolic representations like the double-headed eagle, dating back to the Tsardom period, remain featured in Russia's coat of arms and heraldry. The Russian Bear and Mother Russia are often used as national personifications, and Matryoshka dolls are celebrated as cultural icons of Russia.

Russia's cultural landscape is as diverse as its geography, with traditions deeply rooted in its history. Celebrations like New Year's Day and Orthodox Christmas are widely revered, while Defender of the Fatherland Day and International Women's Day have unique cultural significance. Victory Day is particularly notable, marked by grand parades in Moscow.

The nation's artistic heritage is rich, with early Russian icons by Andrei Rublev evolving to the romantic works of Ivan Aivazovsky and the critical realism of Ilya Repin. In architecture, the transition from wooden structures to the grandeur of the Winter Palace and the iconic onion domes reflects Russia's varied history.

Musically, Russia has been a powerhouse, with Tchaikovsky's Romantic compositions and Stravinsky's avant-garde innovations. Literature boasts giants like Tolstoy and Dostoevsky, whose profound works have left indelible marks on global literature. Russian cuisine, known for its diverse breads and hearty soups like borsch, is complemented by traditional drinks like kvass and vodka.

In media and cinema, Russia has made significant contributions, from news agencies like TASS to pioneering filmmakers like Sergei Eisenstein. Sports are a source of national pride, with achievements in football, ice hockey, and gymnastics highlighting Russia's athletic prowess, despite the shadow of doping controversies. This rich tapestry of holidays, art, music, literature, cuisine, media, and sports paints a vivid picture of Russia's unique and enduring cultural identity.

APPLY YOUR KNOWLEDGE

1. China and Russia are both countries with large territories. State some geographical similarities and differences between the two countries.

2. What is your impression about Russian people? How do you think their characteristics are formed?

# 3.2 Political System

Russian politics operate under a federal semi-presidential system. The President, as head of state, appoints the Prime Minister with parliamentary approval. Executive power lies with the government, while legislative power is held by the Federal Assembly's two houses, supplemented by presidential and governmental regulations. After the Soviet Union's collapse in 1991, Russia struggled to establish a stable political system, culminating in the 1993 constitutional crisis where President Boris Yeltsin dissolved the parliament. A new constitution, strengthening the presidency, was approued by referendum in December 1993. Since then, despite initial regional autonomy, President Vladimir Putin's reforms have centralized federal control, especially over the 22 Republics.

## 3.2.1 The President

The President of Russia plays a crucial role in shaping the country's domestic and foreign policies and acts as the state's representative both domestically and internationally. This includes the appointment and recall of ambassadors, after consulting the legislature, and the authority to conduct international negotiations and sign treaties.

The Constitution adopted in 1993 introduced safeguards against the easy legislative removal of the President. For impeachment on grounds of serious crimes or treason, a complex process is required, involving the State Duma, the Federation Council, and rulings by the Supreme and Constitutional Courts. Removal requires a substantial vote in the Federation Council, and charges lapse if not addressed within three months.

If the President is incapacitated or removed, the Prime Minister temporarily assumes presidential duties until an election is held. The constitution, however, lacks provisions for a vice president and specific criteria for presidential incapacitation.

The President holds significant influence over the government, having the power to appoint and if necessary, dismiss the Prime Minister and government members. The President also plays a key role in appointing key judicial positions, the chairman of the Central Bank, with necessary approvals from the State Duma and the Federation Council, as well as appointing, and federal district court justices.

Russian presidential elections are governed by the constitution and supplementary laws, setting a six-year term limit and allowing only two consecutive terms for a president. Candidates must be Russian citizens, at least 35 years old, and residents of Russia for a minimum of ten years. If the presidency becomes vacant due to health issues, resignation, impeachment, or death, an election must occur within three months, with the Federation Council deciding the date.

The 1995 Law on Presidential Elections, replacing Yeltsin's administration's draft, introduced significant changes from the 1990 election law, including lowering the required signatures for candidate registration. This law aimed to democratize the electoral process, mandating broad regional support for candidates and setting stringent standards for fair campaigning and vote. To be valid, an election required at least 50% voter participation, with provisions to facilitate voting and ensure transparency.

The president must gain over 50% of votes to win; otherwise, a runoff between the top two candidates occurs. The Central Electoral Commission can also disqualify candidates for advocating unconstitutional changes or violating the nation's integrity.

The 1996 election, marked by a contest between Yeltsin and the Communist Party of the Russian Federation (KPRF), was significant in Russian politics. Despite initial low popularity, Yeltsin's vigorous campaign, supported by media and PR experts, including from the United States, led to his victory over KPRF's Gennady Zyuganov. The election, observed internationally and deemed fair, was pivotal in reinforcing Russia's commitment to democratization and regularly contested elections. Yeltsin's re-election campaign was notable for its responsiveness to public opinion and extensive personal engagement across Russia.

During the 1996 election, the presidential role was debated, with some candidates viewing it as overly authoritative, while Yeltsin argued for the necessity of a strong and centralized power. The President's authority extends to issuing decrees that have legal force but must not contravene the constitution or federal laws, subject to constitutional and legal conformity, and even dissolving the State Duma under specific conditions. The President also has the power to call referendums, submit legislative proposals, and enact federal laws.

### 3.2.2 Government

The Russian Government, mirroring a typical Western cabinet structure, consists of the Prime Minister, Deputy Prime Ministers, and Federal Ministers, along with their respective ministries and departments. The Prime Minister, appointed by the President and approved by the State Duma, is responsible for nominating other government officials, including deputy prime ministers and federal ministers. This administration operates according to the constitution, laws, and presidential decrees.

As of mid-1996, the Government comprised 24 ministries responsible for various state functions such as finance, defense, foreign affairs, law enforcement, and civil rights protection. The President has the authority to annul any government decrees conflicting with existing legislation or presidential orders.

The Government's responsibilities include drafting the federal budget and presenting it to the State Duma. Following the parliament's demand in 1994, Government must also provide quarterly reports on budget expenditures. If the State Duma rejects a proposed budget, it goes to a conciliation commission for resolution.

In addition to the ministries, the executive branch in 1996 encompasses 11 state committees and 46 state services and agencies, including the Russian Space Agency and the State Committee for Statistics. The Prime Minister's office, led by Viktor Chernomyrdin at the time, was reported to have around 2,000 staff members.

## 3.2.3 Legislative Branch

Russia's legislative branch, known as the Federal Assembly, is a bicameral parliament comprising the State Duma (the lower house) with 450 members, and the Federation Council (the upper house) with 178 members. Established by the 1993 constitution, the Federal Assembly's structure was set during a referendum in December 1993, concurrent with the first legislative elections. Initially, these Duma deputies served a "transitional" two-year term.

In 1994, a "Civic Accord" was signed by politicians and various leaders, pledging non-violence and constitutional adherence during the transition. The first legislative elections under the new constitution were slightly irregular, with some regions like Tatarstan and Chechnya not participating, leading to incomplete initial membership in the Federation Council. By mid-1994, all positions were filled except for Chechnya.

The Federal Assembly operates continuously, marking a departure from the brief sessions of Soviet-era legislatures. The two houses meet separately, focusing on different legislative areas. State Duma deputies are full-time legislators and cannot hold government roles simultaneously. The Federal Assembly of 1994—1995 was productive, passing numerous laws and working on filling gaps in legislation, particularly in updating civil codes to support a market economy.

The composition and role of the Federation Council, which represents Russia's subnational jurisdictions, has evolved. Legislation in late 1995 formalized its structure, providing ex-officio seats to heads of local legislatures and administrations, totaling 178 seats. The Federation Council, initially composed of many Yeltsin appointees, saw a shift towards elected executives filling its ranks.

Both houses elect chairs and form committees for legislative and oversight functions. The Federation Council has fewer committees due to its part-time nature. In 1996, the composition of these committees largely carried over from the previous parliament.

The State Duma holds significant legislative power, including confirming the Prime Minister. However, its ability to force government resignation is limited, as the president can dissolve the Duma under certain circumstances. The legislative process involves drafts originating from various sources, including the president, government, or the courts. These drafts undergo readings in the State Duma, consideration by the Federation Council, and eventual approval or veto by the President.

The State Duma has the authority to override a presidential veto with a two-thirds majority, a constitutional check on presidential power. The Federal Assembly has some control over finances, but this is limited by requirements for government concurrence on fiscal legislation. This structure establishes a balance of power between the legislative and executive branches in Russian governance.

### 3.2.4 Judiciary Branch

The Russian judicial system, as outlined by the constitution and law, was hierarchically structured with the Constitutional Court, Supreme Court, and, until its 2014 merger, the Supreme Arbitration Court at the top. The system primarily operates through district courts, which handle criminal trials, and regional courts, which serve as appellate courts. Judicial governance involves the All-Russian Congress of Judges and the Council of Judges, supported by the Judicial Department of the Supreme Court, Judicial Qualification Collegia, the Ministry of Justice, and court chairpersons. Despite the presence of various court officers, including jurors, the Prosecutor-General remains a dominant figure in the system.

Many judges, appointed during the eras of Leonid Brezhnev and Yuri Andropov and trained in socialist law, often prioritized political directives over legal principles. Judges, reliant on the Ministry of Justice for infrastructure support and local authorities for housing, faced financial constraints, with salaries typically lower than many other professions. This, combined with appointment irregularities and the influence of procurators, limited the independence of lower jurisdiction judges.

The Constitutional Court, reestablished in March 1995 after being suspended in 1993, played a crucial role in resolving disputes between government branches and between Moscow and regional governments. It also deals with constitutional rights violations, appeals, and presidential impeachment proceedings. However, the 1994 Law on the Constitutional Court restricts its autonomy and the range of issues it can address.

Judicial reforms passed in 2001, including a new Criminal Procedure Code, marked a significant step towards aligning Russia's system with Western models and advancing human rights. These reforms reintroduced jury trials for certain criminal cases and established a more adversarial trial system, better protecting defendants' rights. The 2002 implementation of the new code reduced pretrial detention times and lowered the number of suspects held in pretrial detention. Additionally, it transferred the authority to issue search and arrest warrants from the Procuracy to the courts, further enhancing judicial independence.

### 3.2.5 Regional and Local Administration

Russia's diverse nationalities, numbering around 100, were variously accommodated; some were granted ethnic enclaves with certain federal rights, while others, particularly smaller or more scattered groups, received no such recognition. In these enclaves, ethnic Russians often formed majorities, but the titular nationalities typically had greater representation in local governments. The relationships between the central government, these jurisdictions, and amongst them became more politically significant in the 1990 s.

The 1993 constitution set up a federal structure with eighty-nine subnational jurisdictions, including twenty-one republics for specific ethnic groups, one autonomous regions, the Jewish Autonomous Oblast, six territories, forty-nine oblasts (provinces), and the cities of Moscow and St. Petersburg, each functioning as an independent jurisdiction. Over time, the influence of the central government has waned, elevating the roles of governors and mayors.

The Federation Treaty, signed in March 1992, was an attempt by President Yeltsin to formalize relationships with autonomous republics and other subunits. It categorized regional jurisdictions and outlined their powers, shared powers, and powers reserved for the federal center. Initially supplemented the 1978 constitution, these provisions were demoted upon the ratification of the 1993 constitution, which favored centralizing power.

The 1993 constitution assigns a broad array of powers to the federal center and fewer to joint federal-local authority. Local jurisdictions primarily manage local matters not explicitly controlled by the federal government. The boundaries between federal and local powers remain vague, often clarified through practice or bilateral agreements. Despite constitutional efforts to treat all subunits equally, disparities remain, especially in language rights and the definition of regional categories. The constitution's ambiguity has allowed for flexible conflict resolution.

Bilateral treaties have emerged as a key mechanism for defining the shared powers between the central government and the regions. Notable examples include the 1994 treaty with Tatarstan and subsequent agreements with various oblasts, providing for economic policy sharing, tax control, and other regional autonomies.

By the mid-1990s, regional governments began enacting local legislation to address issues in the absence of federal statutes. This autonomy is upheld by the constitution, provided regional laws align with it and existing federal laws.

Throughout Yeltsin's presidency, 46 power-sharing treaties were signed, granting varying degrees of autonomy to different regions. However, under President Vladimir Putin, these agreements began to be abolished or expired, marking a shift towards centralization and the reduction of regional autonomies. By 2017, the last of these treaties had expired, signifying the end of this period of regional autonomy.

APPLY YOUR KNOWLEDGE

1. How has the 1993 constitution impacted the balance of power between the Russian presidency and the Federal Assembly?

2. What effect have President Putin's reforms had on the autonomy of the 22 Republics within the Russian Federation?

# 3.3 Economy

Russia's economy, once a planned system, has evolved into a market-oriented mixed economy, rich in natural resources like oil and natural gas. As of 2023, it ranked as the world's 11th largest economy based on nominal GDP, 5th in terms of purchasing power parity (PPP) as per the International Monetary Fund (IMF), and 5th according to the World Bank. However, due to fluctuating currency exchange rates, Russia's GDP in dollar terms varies significantly. Russia became a member of the World Trade Organization (WTO) in 2012.

The country's vast and diverse geography plays a key role in its economic activities, particularly in terms of natural resource availability. Russia is often called an Energy Superpower because it has the world's largest natural gas reserves, the second-largest coal reserves, the eighth-largest oil reserves, and Europe's largest oil shale reserves. It leads globally in natural gas exports, ranks second in natural gas production but third in oil production, and is the third largest coal exporter. Russia's foreign exchange reserves are among the world's largest, its workforce of approximately 70 million, making it the seventh-largest globally. The country ranks as the word's second-largest arms exporter.

The oil and gas sector significantly contributes to Russia's federal budget revenues and exports, accounted for around 34% of the federal budget and 54% of exports in 2021. Russia also has a notable number of billionaires, ranking seventh globally in billionaire count. However, income and wealth inequality in Russia remain relatively high.

## 3.3.1 Historical Background

The Russian economy has experienced significant changes after 1991, transitioning from a socialist command system to a mixed market economy. This shift led to a move away from heavy manufacturing and agriculture, favoring services, oil, gas, and mining industries. According to Richard Connolly, four key traits have shaped Russia's economy over the last four centuries: A weak legal system with unreliable courts and contracts; the dominance of basic agriculture until the 1950s; technological backwardness, slightly mitigated by borrowing from the West; and lower living standards compared to Western

Europe and North America.

In the late 19th century, Russia underwent critical reforms to maintain its global power and influence. This period saw the abolition of serfdom addressing the crisis in the landlord economy, the poverty of peasants, and the lack of a developed domestic market and wage labor.

The economy guided by five-year plans from 1928, transitioned from an agrarian to an industrial society by the 1950s. By the 1970s, the Union experienced stagnation due to overburdened central planners and an inflexible administrative system. In the mid-1980s, Mikhail Gorbachev's Perestroika reforms to move towards a market-oriented economy ultimately failed.

Russia's shift to a market economy saw rapid privatization, often corrupt, leading to economic collapse, hyperinflation, and widespread poverty. The "shock therapy" reforms, aimed at rapid market liberalization, resulted in a 40% GDP drop between 1999 and 1996, and significant social and economic inequality.

Russia's economy recovered from the 1998 financial crisis, benefiting from devalued currency and rising commodity prices. Major reforms in the early 2000s, including tax and deregulation measures, contributed to economic growth, with GDP growing 6.7% per year on average.

In 2008, Russia's economy faced challenges from the global financial crisis but recovered by late 2009. Despite significant gains, income and wealth remained unevenly distributed.

Western sanctions impacted the Russian economy, leading to a decline in the ruble's value. However, Russia's low import dependence and large reserves in natural resources, such as oil and gas, provided some economic resilience.

The ruble's value began to fall in 2023, with increasing inflation and a projected budget deficit. Russia's economy continues to face uncertainty amid ongoing geopolitical tensions and global economic shifts.

### 3.3.2 Energy

Russia, rich in natural resources due to its extensive Ural Mountains and the immense reserves of oil, gas, coal, and timber in Siberia and the Russian Far East, is a major player in global energy markets. Although it was a key supplier until 2022, the country's economy significantly relies on its energy exports, especially oil and gas, which are a major source of foreign currency.

Russia is known as an Energy Superpower, holding the world's largest reserves of natural gas, the second-largest reserves of coal, the sixth-largest oil reserves, and the largest oil shale reserves in Europe. It leads globally as the top exporter of natural gas, ranks second in oil production while leading in natural gas exports, and is the third-largest coal exporter. Russia also contributes significantly to greenhouse gas emissions due to its reliance on fossil fuels.

The country is a major electricity producer, ranking fourth globally, and was also among the leaders in renewable energy production in 2019. Notably, Russia pioneered civilian nuclear power, developing the first nuclear power plant, and as of 2019, was the third-largest producer of nuclear energy. Rosatom, Russia's state nuclear conglomerate, plays a dominant role in the international nuclear power market.

In terms of economic impact, the oil and gas sector accounted for about 20% of Russia's GDP in the mid-2000s and around 20% ~ 21% in 2013. This sector also represents about half of Russia's exports and federal budget revenues. However, Russia's GDP dynamics are heavily influenced by oil and gas prices, although the sector's share in GDP is less than 50%. A comprehensive assessment by Rosstat in 2021 reported that the total share of the oil and gas sector, including all related activities, ranged from 15.2% to 21.1% of GDP between 2017 and 2020.

Domestically, Russia consumes two-thirds of its gas production and a quarter of its oil production. It exports three-quarters of its oil, holding a significant share of the global oil market. Despite the importance of oil and gas revenues, experts note that the total contribution of these sectors to Russia's GDP might be higher when considering indirect revenues and expenditures in the economy.

In 2023, Russia experienced a 24% decrease in oil and gas tax revenues compared to the previous year, totaling 8.8 trillionroubles (approximately $96.2 billion).

### 3.3.3 Mining

Russia is a global leader in the mining industry, known for producing and exporting a wide range of minerals, notably diamonds, gold, and platinum. It's the world's top diamond-producing country, with an estimated production of over 33 million carats in

2013, making up 25% of the global output and valued at around $3.4 billion. The state-owned company ALROSA is dominates approximately 95% of all Russian diamond production.

In the realm of precious metals, Russia ranks third globally in gold production and second in platinum production. It's also a significant producer of silver, holding the fourth spot worldwide. Beyond precious metals, Russia is prominent in the production of various other minerals.

(1) Copper: 9th largest producer worldwide.

(2) Nickel: 3rd largest producer globally.

(3) Lead: 6th largest producer in the world.

(4) Bauxite: 9th largest producer globally.

(5) Zinc: 10th largest producer in the world.

(6) Vanadium and Cobalt: 2nd largest producer of both globally.

(7) Iron Ore: 5th largest producer worldwide.

(8) Boron: 7th largest producer in the world.

(9) Molybdenum: 9th largest producer globally.

(10) Tin: 13th largest producer worldwide.

(11) Sulfur: 3rd largest producer globally.

(12) Phosphate: 4th largest producer in the world.

(13) Gypsum: 8th largest producer globally.

(14) Salt: 10th largest producer in the world.

(15) Uranium: 6th largest producer as of 2018.

This diverse range of mineral production underscores Russia's significant role in the global mining industry.

## 3.3.4 Agriculture

Agriculture is a significant sector in Russia, contributing about 5% to the national GDP and employing around 12.5% of the labor force. The country boasts the third-largest cultivated area in the world, spanning approximately 1,265,267 square kilometers. However, the challenging climate means that only about 15.3% of Russia's land is dedicated to agriculture, and just 7.4% is arable.

Grain is the cornerstone of Russian agriculture, occupying more than half of the cropland. Russia stands as the world's largest wheat exporter and holds a leading position in the production of other grains such as barley, buckwheat, oats, and rye. It's also the second-largest producer of sunflower seeds. Climate change adaptation could potentially enhance agricultural opportunities in Russia, particularly in Siberia, attracting both internal and external migration to the region for farming.

Aside from grains, over one-third of Russia's sown area is allocated for fodder crops, with the remaining land used for industrial crops, vegetables, and fruits. With its vast coastline stretching across three oceans, Russia also has a significant presence in the global fishing industry. It ranks sixth in the world in terms of fish caught, with a total catch of 5,021,000 tons in 2023. Russia is renowned for its high-quality beluga caviar and is a major producer of canned fish, contributing around one-third of the world's supply. Additionally, it accounts for about a quarter of the global market for fresh and frozen fish.

## 3.3.5 Industry

Russia's defense industry is a key sector and a significant employer. It is highly advanced in designing and producing sophisticated military equipment, such as fifth-generation fighter jets, nuclear submarines, various firearms, and ballistic missiles. As the world's second-largest arms exporter, Russia is only surpassed by the United States in arms sales globally.

The aerospace industry, including both military and civilian sectors, is vital for Russia, employing about 355,300 people. Russia's aircraft industry is known for its internationally competitive military aircraft, like the MiG-29 and Su-30. Civil aviation projects like the Sukhoi Superjet 100 aim to rejuvenate the civilian sector. In 2009, the United Aircraft Corporation delivered 95 new aircraft, including 15 civilian models, and over 141 helicopters. This industry is one of Russia's most science-intensive sectors and a significant employer of skilled personnel, with aircraft products comprising over half of the nation's arms exports.

The automotive industry is a major sector in Russia, directly employing around 600,000 people (0.83% of workforce). In 2018, Russia ranked 13th globally in vehicle production, making 1,767,674 vehicles and accounting for 1.8% of global production. However, following 2022 sanctions and the exit of Western manufacturers, production plummeted to 450,000 passenger cars, the lowest since the Soviet Union's dissolution. Main domestic brands includeAvtoVAZ and GAZ for light vehicles, and KamAZ for heavy vehicles. As of December 2022, the industry is largely supported by Chinese manufacturers.

Russia was experiencing growth in microelectronics, particularly with the development of Mikron JSC. However, this resurgence faced challenges following sanctions in 2022.

### 3.3.6 Services

As of 2013, Russians have spent a high percentage of their pre-tax income on shopping, often in shopping malls, partly due to high homeownership rates. In 2020, Russia had over 1,000 shopping malls, but the 2022 international company exodus left many stores empty. Supermarkets are typical anchor stores in Russian malls. There has been a steady growth in retail sales over the years, reaching 42.51 trillion RUB in 2022.

Russia's telecommunications sector has grown significantly, with a strong presence of broadband, mobile networks, and internet users. As of 2020, 85% of Russians used the internet. The country has four major national mobile phone networks with substantial subscriptions.

Russian Railways dominates railway transport, with the country boasting the third-longest railway tracks globally. Russia has a vast network of roads and inland waterways, numerous airports with Sheremetyevo International Airport being the busiest, and the largest port in Novorossiysk. It uniquely operates nuclear-powered icebreakers, enhancing Arctic trade via the Northern Sea Route.

In 2022, the construction industry was valued at 13 trillion RUB, with a significant focus on residential construction. Goals for 2020—2030 include extensive housing projects and renovations.

Russia's insurance market features over 400 companies, with significant business concentration across major segments. The market has grown notably in operations, with an increase in premiums and claims paid.

Russia's IT sector is dynamic, benefiting from a high number of academic graduates. The government supports IT development through technology parks and initiatives to increase domestic technology use in state-owned companies.

Russia is a popular tourist destination, ranking sixteenth globally in visits. Key attractions include historical sites and landmarks like thePeterhof Palace, Red Square, and the Trans-Siberian Railway.

APPLY YOUR KNOWLEDGE

1. How did the shift from a planned to a market-oriented economy affect Russia's major industries like energy and mining?

2. What are the immediate and potential long-term impacts of the 2022 sanctions on Russia's international trade and energy exports?

## AFTER CLASS

### KEY TERMS

Ural Mountains
Lake Baikal
Eastern Orthodox Christianity
Matryoshka
Soviet Union
Federal semi-presidential system
Tchaikovsky
State Duma
Federation Council

### EXTENSION

● Russian Literature and Music

Russian culture, rich in history and depth, has profoundly influenced the world through its literature and music, reflecting the nation's soul and its evolving social dynamics. In literature, giants like Leo Tolstoy and Fyodor Dostoevsky explored complex human emotions and ethical dilemmas in works such as "*War and Peace*" and "*Crime and Punishment*". Anton Chekhov, with his nuanced portrayals in short stories and plays, emphasized character and atmosphere, setting a new standard for Russian drama.

Maxim Gorky, another monumental figure, became a transitional figure between pre-revolutionary and Soviet literary. His works, including "*The Lower Depths*" and "*Mother*", delve into the lives of the lower classes and the rise of revolutionary sentiments, making him a key figure in the development of Socialist Realism in literature.

During the Soviet era, literature adapted to new roles, often promoting state ideologies while also offering subtle critiques. Nikolai Ostrovsky's "*How Steel Was Tempered*" serves as a quintessential example of socialist realism, portraying the life of Pavel Korchagin, a devoted Bolshevik, whose development mirrors the tempering process of steel—strengthened through adversity. This novel, along with others, motivated and exemplified virtues like perseverance and loyalty to the socialist cause.

In the classical music domain, composers like Pyotr Ilyich Tchaikovsky captivated audiences with "*Swan Lake*" and "*The Nutcracker*". Later, Sergei Rachmaninoff and Igor Stravinsky expanded musical boundaries, while Soviet composers like Dmitri Shostakovich and Sergei Prokofiev navigated the intricacies of innovation, reflecting the complexities of Soviet life in their compositions.

Soviet music also resonated with powerful themes of patriotism and collective effort. Songs like "*Катюша*", a beloved folk song, stirred feelings of nostalgia and national pride. It became synonymous with the spirit of the Russian people during World War Ⅱ, embodying resilience and hope.

CASE STUDIES

●Vladimir Putin: Architect of Modern Russia

Vladimir Putin, a central figure in contemporary Russian politics, has been significantly influenced the country's direction since the turn of the millennium. Born in 1952 in Leningrad (now St. Petersburg), Putin began his career in the KGB, Soviet Union's main security agency. His rise in politics began in the 1990s, culminating in his appointment as Prime Minister in 1999 and his subsequent election as President in 2000.

Under Putin's leadership, Russia has seen a blend of economic growth and political centralization. He is credited with stabilizing the Russian economy following the tumultuous 1990s, largely through leveraging the country's vast natural resources, particularly oil and gas. This economic stability has contributed to a significant improvement in the standard of living for many Russians.

Politically, Putin's tenure has been characterized by a consolidation of power aimed at enhancing stability and coherence. He has introduced policies designed to reinforce federal authority, streamline governance, and ensure a unified national vision. These measures have included efforts to harmonize the influence of regional leaders with federal objectives and to maintain a cohesive narrative through state media, fostering a sense of national unity and purpose.

On the international stage, Putin has worked to reassert Russia as a major global player. His foreign policy actions bolstered his image as a defender of Russian interests.

Putin shaping the country's trajectory and its role on the world stage.

CLASS DISCUSSION

How did Vladimir Putin stabilize the Russian economy following the tumultuous 1990s, and what were the key factors that contributed to this stabilization? Discuss the role of natural resources, particularly oil and gas, in this process and the impact on the standard of living for Russians?

● Russia and the Arctic

The relationship between Russia and the Arctic is of profound strategic importance, driven by the region's vast natural resources and emerging shipping routes from melting ice. With its extensive Arctic coastline and substantial territorial claims, Russia views the Arctic as a cornerstone of its national security and economic strategy.

Russia has prioritized the Arctic for its rich deposits of oil, gas, and minerals, increasingly accessible with declining ice recedes. The Northern Sea Route (NSR), running along the Russian Arctic coast, is central to Russia's strategy. The NSR offers a shorter maritime route between Europe and Asia, potentially transforming global shipping by reducing travel time and costs. Russia has invested heavily in Arcticinfrastructure, including ports, icebreakers, and search and rescue capabilities, to support this route.

Economic development in the Arctic is vital for Russia, especially given sanctions and economic pressures. Major projects like the Yamal liquefied natural gas (LNG) development showcase Russia's commitment to exploiting Arctic resources. These projects aim to boost energy exports and attract foreign investment and technological expertise. The Russian government has introduced incentives and regulatory frameworks to facilitate Arctic exploration and development.

The Arctic environment presents significant challenges, including harsh weather, ice navigation hazards, and environmental protection concerns. Russia's strategy includes building advanced icebreaker fleets and implementing strict environmental regulations. However, balancing economic activities with environmental sustainability remains complex, particularly as climate change accelerates the region's transformation.

Geopolitically, the Arctic is becoming a focal point for international competition. Russia's assertive stance is partly driven by the desire to secure its territorial claims and strategic interests. Increased Russian military presence and infrastructure reflect these concerns. Despite the competitive nature of Arctic geopolitics, international cooperation remains crucial. Russia participates in the Arctic Council, promoting collaboration on environmental protection, sustainable development, and scientific research.

● How does Russia's investment in Arctic infrastructure, such as ports, icebreakers, and search and rescue capabilities, support its economic strategy? Discuss the role of the Northern Sea Route (NSR) in this context and the potential benefits for global shipping.

FOR FUN

1. Website to visit

(1) Russia Beyond (rbth. com)

(2) The Moscow Times

2. Video to watch

(1) "Russia: Land of the Tsars"

(2) "Ballet in the Bolshoi Theatre"

(3) "Russian Ark"

3. Works to read

(1) "Opportunity thrive for Northeast China, Russia's Far East" from China Daily

(2) "*The Russian Soul: What Does It Mean?*" by Anastasia Stognei

# Unit 4 Regions as Context: Cases from the United States

The United States is the only country in the world that went from barbarism to decadence without civilization in between.

—Oscar Wilde

We are and always will be a nation of immigrants. We were strangers once, too.

—Barack Obama

## LEARNING OUTCOMES

■ Explain the basic characteristics of the geography of the United States, including its diverse topography, varied climate zones, and extensive natural resources.

■ Identify the diversity of ethnic groups and a large immigrant population that shape cultural and social values inthe United States.

■ State the features of the political system of the United States and its changing complexity.

■ Describe the structure of U. S. economy and its position in the world.

■ Summarize the foreign relations ofthe United States and describe how its foreign policies impact global affairs.

## BEFORE CLASS

■ Resource 1 9 Stereotypes All Americans Hate(theculturetrip. com)

■ Resource 2 10 Things to Know About U. S. Culture | InterExchange

■ Resource 3 American culture: United States traditions and Customs | Live Science

After you read the above materials, please answer the following questions.

1. How do you summarize the national character of the United States?

2. In terms of national character, what are the major differences between Chinese

and Americans?

3. What are the common stereotypes towards Americans?

4. How do you think these characters and stereotypes are formed?

# 4.1 Land & People

## 4.1.1 Geography

The United States ranks among the world's largest countries by land area. Its territory covers an area of approximately 9.8 million square kilometers according to different ways of measurement.

The country's geography varies widely. Along the Atlantic coast, there are flat plains that transition into forests and hills further inland, known as the Piedmont region.

Moving inland, the Appalachian Mountains and the Adirondack are part of the Appalachian system from the Great Lakes and the Midwest grasslands. The Mississippi River, one of the world's longest river systems, flows primarily southward through the central part of the country.

To the west, the Great Plains feature vast stretches of flat, fertile land, with some highland areas in the southeast. Beyond the Great Plains lie the Rocky Mountains, reaching heights of over 14,000 feet in Colorado. Further west, there are Rocky regions like the Great Basin and various deserts such as the Chihuahua Desert, Sonoran, and Mojave.

Along the Pacific coast, the Sierra Nevada and Cascade mountain ranges run parallel. The lowest and highest points in the contiguous United States are both found in California, about 84 miles apart. The highest peak in the country and continent is Denali in Alaska, standing at 20,310 feet.

Alaska also hosts numerous active volcanoes in the Alexander and Aleutian Islands, while Hawaii consists of volcanic islands. The Yellowstone National Park, located in the Rockies, is home to the continent's largest supervolcano.

As of 2021, the United States contained 11% of the world's permanent meadows and pastures and 10% of cropland.

## 4.1.2 People

Americans are often described as diverse and dynamic, reflecting the vast array of cultural, ethnic, and historical influences that have shaped the nation. This diversity is evident not just in the demographic makeup but also in the varied lifestyles, beliefs, and values across the country. Generally, Americans are known for their spirit of independence, innovation, and a strong sense of individualism. They value personal freedom and are often seen as forward-thinking and optimistic.

Socially, Americans are known for their openness and friendliness. They tend to value community involvement and are known for their philanthropic spirit, often volunteering and donating to causes. This generosity is a hallmark of American civic life.

Culturally, the United States is a melting pot where various cultures blend yet retain distinctive traits. This cultural diversity is celebrated through numerous ethnic festivals, culinary traditions, and artistic expressions. The influence of immigrants on American culture is profound, continually reshaping the cultural landscape.

Economically, Americans are often characterized as entrepreneurial and hardworking. The American Dream, the idea that anyone can achieve success through hard work and determination, still resonates strongly and attracts immigrants seeking opportunity.

Despite these general traits, it's crucial to acknowledge the significant regional differences within the country, from the conservative, traditional values often found in the Southern "Bible Belt" to the more liberal, progressive attitudes typical of coastal urban areas like New York and San Francisco. These regional variations add to the complex, multifaceted nature of American identity.

As of April 1, 2020, the U. S. Census Bureau recorded a population of 331,449,281 inhabitants, positioning the United States as the world's third-most populous nation, following China and India. According to the U. S. Population Clock data from January 28, 2021, the population of the United States has been experiencing a net increase of one person every 100 seconds, equivalent to approximately 864 individuals per day. In 2018, statistics indicated that 52% of Americans aged 15 and older were married, while 6% were widowed, 10% were divorced, and 32% had never been married. Moreover, the total fertility rate in the United States in 2021 was reported at 1.7 children per woman. Additionally, the country had the highest proportion of children (23%) living in single-parent households in 2019.

| Ancestry Group | Percentage of Total Population |
|---|---|
| White Americans | 57.8% |
| Hispanic and Latino Americans | 18.7% |
| African Americans | 12.1% |
| Asian Americans | 5.9% |
| Native Americans | Approximately 1% |

The United States boasts a richly diverse population, encompassing 37 ancestry groups, each with over one million members. White Americans tracing their roots to Europe, the Middle East, or North Africa, constitute the largest racial and ethnic group, comprising 57.8% of the population. Following closely are Hispanic and Latino Americans, constituting 18.7% of the total population. African Americans rank as the country's third-largest ancestry group, representing 12.1% of the U. S. population. Asian Americans form the fourth-largest group, making up 5.9% of the population, while Native Americans, totaling 3.7 million individuals, account for approximately 1%. As of 2020, the median age of the United States population stood at 38.5 years.

## 4.1.3 Language

In the United States, a multitude of languages is spoken, but English reigns supreme as the most widely spoken and written language. Although there is no official language at the federal level, certain laws, such as those governing U. S. naturalization requirements, promote the standardization of English. Additionally, most states have designated English as the official language.

However, three states and four U. S. territories have acknowledged local or indigenous languages alongside English. These include Hawaii (Hawaiian), Alaska (twenty Native languages), South Dakota (Sioux as indigenous language), American Samoa (Samoan), Puerto Rico (Spanish), Guam (Chamorro), and the Northern Mariana Islands (Carolinian and Chamorro). In Puerto Rico particularly, Spanish enjoys broader usage compared to English.

According to the American Community Survey conducted in 2010, approximately 229 million individuals out of the total U. S. population of 308 million spoke only English at home. Spanish ranked as the second most commonly spoken language, with around 37 million speakers at home. Other languages spoken by one million people or more included Chinese (2. 8 million), Tagalog (1. 6 million), Vietnamese (1. 4 million), French (1. 3 million), Korean (1. 1 million), and German (1 million).

The immigrant population of the United States, totaling 51 million, stands as the largest in the world in absolute terms. As of 2022, the country hosted 87. 7 million immigrants and U. S. -born children of immigrants, representing nearly 27% of the total U. S. population. Among the foreign-born population in 2017, approximately 45% (20. 7 million) held naturalized citizenship, while 27% (12. 3 million) were lawful permanent residents, 6% (2. 2 million) held temporary lawful residency, and 23% (10. 5 million) were unauthorized immigrants.

In terms of origin countries, Mexico accounted for the largest share of immigrants in 2019, constituting 24% of the immigrant population, followed by India (6%), China (5%), the Philippines (4. 5%), and El Salvador (3%). For decades, the United States has been at the forefront of refugee resettlement efforts, admitting more refugees than the rest of the world combined.

### 4.1.4 Religion and Culture

The First Amendment of the United States Constitution guarantees the free exercise of religion and prohibits Congress from enacting laws respecting its establishment. Religious practice in the United States is widespread and diverse, contributing to a profoundly vibrant religious landscape that is among the most varied in the world. With the world's largest Christian population, the country also hosts a significant portion of the global Jewish population under the Law of Return.

In addition to Christianity and Judaism, other notable faiths include Buddhism, Hinduism, Islam, various New Age Movements, and Native American religions. Religious practices vary significantly by region, with evangelical Protestantism holding cultural significance in the "Bible Belt" of the Southern United States, while regions like New England and the Western United States tend to be more secular.

Despite regional variations, the overwhelming majority of Americans believe in a higher power or spiritual force, engage in spiritual practices such as prayer, and identify themselves as religious or spiritual individuals. "Ceremonial deism", a concept where religious references and practices are intertwined with secular culture, is common in American society.

Americans traditionally embrace a unifying political ideology known as the "American creed", which emphasizes principles such as liberty, equality under the law, democracy, social equality, property rights, and a preference for limited government. Culturally, the nation is characterized by values of individualism, personal autonomy, a strong work ethic, competitiveness, and voluntary altruism towards others. In fact, Americans have demonstrated exceptional generosity, as evidenced by their substantial charitable contributions, which amounted to 1.44% of gross national income (GNI) according to a 2016 study by the Charities Aid Foundation, the highest rate globally by a significant margin.

The United States is a melting pot of diverse ethnic groups, traditions, and values, with significant cultural and economic influence worldwide. While the majority of present Americans or their ancestors originated from Europe, Africa, and Asia within the last five centuries, mainstream American culture is predominantly rooted in Western traditions brought over by European immigrants, albeit with influences from various other sources, including African traditions introduced by enslaved individuals. More recent immigration from Asia and Latin America has contributed to a cultural tapestry that is often described as both assimilative and heterogeneous, with immigrants contributing to and adapting to mainstream American culture. The allure of the American Dream, which promotes the idea of high social mobility, has historically attracted immigrants, although the accuracy of this perception remains a subject of debate.

Despite the notion of a classless society in mainstream culture, scholars identify significant differences between social classes in the United States, impacting socialization, language, and values. While socioeconomic achievement is highly esteemed, there is also recognition of the dignity in being ordinary or average.

The United States is widely regarded as having robust protections for free speech under the First Amendment, encompassing controversial forms of expression such as flag desecration, hate speech, blasphemy, and defamation of public figures.

APPLY YOUR KNOWLEDGE

1. How does the United States' geographic diversity influence its regional economic activities and cultural identities?

2. How does the diversity of ethnic groups and a large immigrant population shape American cultural and social values, including the concept of the "American Dream"?

# 4.2 Political System

## 4.2.1 Federal Government

The United States is a federal republic comprising 50 states, with its capital situated in a federal district. It exercises sovereignty over five unincorporated territories and several uninhabited island possessions, with certain island claims are subject to dispute.

Functioning as a liberal representative democracy, the United States upholds the principle of majority rule tempered by minority rights protected by law. The Constitution of the United States stands as the nation's paramount legal document, delineating the structure and responsibilities of the federal government and its relationship with the individual states.

Comprising three branches, all based in Washington, D. C., the federal government serves as the national governing body of the United States, upheld by a robust system of checks and balances.

The U. S. Congress, a bicameral legislature consisting of the Senate and the House of Representatives, holds the authority to enact federal laws, declare war, ratify treaties, control government spending, and initiate impeachment proceedings. The Senate comprises 100 members, with each state represented by two senators serving six-year terms, while the House of Representatives consists of 435 members elected from single-member congressional districts based on population, serving two-year terms.

The President of the United States serves as the commander-in-chief of the military, possesses the power to veto legislative bills (which can be overridden by Congress), and appoints cabinet members and other officials to execute and enforce federal laws and policies through their respective agencies. Voter elect the president and vice president jointly via the Electoral College. They serve a four-year term with a maximum of two terms.

The U. S. federal judiciary, including the Supreme Court, courts of appeals, and district courts, is responsible for interpreting laws and adjudicating disputes. Judges are appointed for life by the president with Senate approval. The Supreme Court, led by the chief justice of the United States and consisting of nine members, holds the authority to overturn laws deemed unconstitutional.

This three-branch system, known as the presidential system, contrasts with the parliamentary system, where the executive is a part of the legislative body. The framework established by the U. S. Constitution in 1789 has been emulated by numerous countries worldwide, particularly in the Americas.

Although the Constitution does not explicitly mention political parties, they emerged independently in the late 18th century with the formation of the Federalist and Anti-Federalist parties. Since then, the United States has effectively operated as a two-party system, with different parties dominating at various times.

The two principal national parties are currently the Democratic and Republican parties. The Democratic Party is generally perceived as more liberal in its political platform, while the Republican Party is seen as more conservative. Each party maintains a primary system to nominate candidates for the presidential ticket and fields candidates for various other offices in every state. While smaller and less influential parties exist, they do not possess the same national scope and influence as the two major parties.

## 4.2.2 Local Governments

In the American federal system, governmental powers are allocated between two levels of elected government: the national government and state governments. Additionally, people within states are represented by local elected governments, which serve as administrative divisions of the states.

States are further subdivided into counties or county-equivalents, and these are then divided into municipalities. The District of Columbia, meanwhile, serves as a federal district housing the capital of the United States, Washington, D. C. Both territories and the District of Columbia function as administrative divisions of the federal government.

In the United States, a state constitutes a fundamental political entity, and there are a total of 50 states. These states are unified within a political union, with each one exercising governmental authority over a distinct and defined geographic area. Within their respective territories, states share sovereignty with the federal government. Consequently, individuals in the United States hold citizenship both at the federal level and within the state where they reside. State citizenship and residency are flexible, allowing for movement between states without the need for government approval, except in cases involving certain legal restrictions such as court-ordered constraints on individuals like paroled convicts or children under shared custody arrangements.

The governance structure of each state is established by its citizens through individual state constitutions. Grounded in republican principles as mandated by the federal constitution, these constitutions provide for a government structure comprising three separate and independent branches: executive, legislative, and judicial. States are further subdivided into counties or county-equivalents, which may possess limited local governmental authority but are not considered sovereign entities. The organization and responsibilities of counties vary significantly across states, with additional local government entities established by states as needed.

Unlike U. S. territories, states possess extensive powers and rights under the United States Constitution. They are represented in the United States Congress, which comprises the Senate and the House of Representatives. Each state also has the privilege of appointing a number of electors equivalent to its total congressional delegation to participate in the Electoral College, which elects the president. States also have the authority to ratify constitutional amendments and, with congressional consent, enter into interstate compacts. Furthermore, the police power of each state is acknowledged.

Traditionally, tasks such as local law enforcement, public education, public health, intrastate commerce regulation, and local transportation and infrastructure have been considered primarily state responsibilities, although federal involvement in these areas has increased over time through funding and regulation. Constitutional amendments and evolving interpretations have led to a trend of centralization, with the federal government assuming a larger role than in the past. Nevertheless, there remains an ongoing debate regarding states'rights, focusing on the extent of states'powers and sovereignty vis-ὰ-vis the federal government and individual rights.

Congress holds the authority to admit new states into the Union, a process that has expanded the original 13 states to the current 50. Each new state is admitted on equal footing with existing states.

## 4.2.3 Military Forces

The United States Armed Forces represent the military might of the nation. Comprising six distinct service branches—the Army, Marine Corps, Navy, Air Force, Space Force; and Coast Guard—these armed services collectively constitute eight uniformed services of the United States.

Each branch of the military is tasked with specific responsibilities and areas of operation. The Army specializes in land operations, while the Navy and Marine Corps focus on maritime activities, with the latter particularly adept at amphibious and littoral operations in support of naval endeavors. Air operations are conducted by the Air Force, while the Space Force handles operations in space. Notably, the Coast Guard stands out as a maritime-focused service with additional responsibilities in law enforcement.

Throughout American history, the U. S. Armed Forces have played pivotal roles in shaping the nation. From their inception during the Revolutionary War to their involvement in significant conflicts like the Civil War, these forces have been instrumental in the country's development. The modern framework of the U. S. military was established by the National Security Act of 1947, creating the Department of Defense (DoD) and consolidating various military branches under its umbrella.

As per the U. S. Constitution, the president serves as the commander-in-chief of the armed forces and collaborates with the DoD and the Department of Homeland Security (DHS) to formulate military policy.

Renowned for their size and capabilities, the U. S. Armed Forces are among the largest in the world, drawing personnel from a pool of dedicated volunteers. While conscription has been utilized in the past, it has not been in effect since 1973, though the Selective Service System maintains the authority to conscript males aged 18 to 25.

With a military expenditure reaching US $877 billion in 2022, the highest globally—the United States boasts formidable defense capabilities and power projection abilities. Advanced technologies, fueled by substantial funding, enable the widespread deployment of U. S. forces worldwide, including the operation of approximately 800 military bases beyond its borders. Domestically, the U. S. Armed Forces include the world's largest air force (Air Force), naval aviation service (Naval Air Forces), and navy (Navy), along with the world's only active independent space force (Space Force) and the 12th-largest maritime force (Coast Guard).

## 4.2.4 Law Enforcement

Law enforcement in the United States is decentralized, with various agencies operating at the local, state, and federal levels. The majority of law enforcement activities are carried out by local police departments and sheriff departments within their respective jurisdictions. These agencies are responsible for maintaining public order, enforcing local ordinances and state laws, and investigating crimes within their communities.

At the state level, there are state police departments that have jurisdiction throughout the entire state. These agencies often handle investigations that cross county lines or require specialized resources. They may also provide support to local law enforcement agencies in certain situations.

Federal law enforcement agencies, such as the Federal Bureau of Investigation (FBI) and the U. S. Marshals Service, have national jurisdiction and focus on enforcing federal laws, protecting national security, and upholding civil rights. These agencies often handle cases involving organized crime, terrorism, cybercrime, and other federal offenses. Additionally, federal agencies may assist state and local authorities in joint investigations or provide resources and expertise when needed.

The criminal justice system in the United States includes both state and federal courts. State courts have jurisdiction over most criminal and civil cases, while federal courts handle cases involving violations of federal laws, interstate crimes, and disputes between parties from different states. Appeals of state court decisions can be heard in federal courts under certain circumstances.

Despite efforts to maintain public safety, the United States faces challenges such as high rates of incarceration and violent crime. The country's incarceration rate is among the highest in the world, and gun-related homicides are significantly more prevalent compared to other high-income countries. Addressing these issues requires comprehensive approaches that involve law enforcement, community engagement, and social programs aimed at preventing crime and promoting public safety.

APPLY YOUR KNOWLEDGE

1. Analyze the checks and balances system in the U. S. government. How does this system impact the relationship between the executive, legislative, and judicial branches?

2. How do local governments fit into the federal structure of the U. S. ? Consider the roles of states, counties, and municipalities in governance and how they interact with federal authority.

# 4. 3 Economy

## 4.3.1 An Overview

The United States boasts a highly developed mixed economy, recognized as the world's largest economy based on nominal GDP and the third largest based on purchasing power parity(PPP), trailing China and European Union in 2024. With the fifth highest per capita GDP(nominal) and the eighth highest per capita GDP(PPP) as of 2024, the U. S. contributes significantly to global economic landscape, accounting for 25. 4% of the global economy in nominal terms and about 15. 6% in PPP terms. The U. S. dollar serves as the predominant currency in international transactions and holds the status of the world's reserve currency, supported by its extensive use in global financial markets, its role as the reference standard for the petrodollar system, and its association with the eurodollar. Numerous countries adopt the U. S. dollar as their official or de facto currency.

The American economy thrives on high productivity levels, well-developed transportation infrastructure, and abundant natural resources. Americans enjoy the highest average household and employee incomes among OECD member states, with the highest median household income recorded in 2021. However, income inequality remains a pressing issue, with the U. S. exhibiting one of the highest levels of income inequality among developed nations. Key trading partners for the U. S. include Canada, Mexico, China, Japan, Germany, South Korea, the United Kingdom, India, and Vietnam. As the world's largest importer and second-largest exporter, the U. S. engages in free trade agreements with several countries, including Canada and Mexico through the USMCA, Australia, South Korea, and Israel, among others.

Historically, the United States has been a powerhouse in global economics, surpassing the British Empire as the most productive economy by 1890. It remains the leading producer of petroleum and natural gas globally, with its manufacturing sector accounting for a significant portion of global output. With a robust internal market for goods and dominance in services trade, the U. S. plays a central role in global trade and commerce. The country hosts the largest number of billionaires worldwide, and its commercial banks and global assets under management reflect its economic prowess. Despite enduring challenges, such as the Great Recession of 2008, the U. S. has demonstrated resilience, implementing measures like the American Reinvestment and Recovery Act to spur economic recovery and achieving the longest recorded U. S. economic expansion on record by July 2019.

The New York Stock Exchange and Nasdaq stand as the world's largest stock exchanges by market capitalization and trade volume, underscoring the significance of the U. S. financial sector. Renowned for its vibrant consumer market, the U. S. economy relies heavily on consumer spending, which comprises a significant portion of GDP. The nation's labor market has attracted immigrants from across the globe, contributing to its dynamic workforce and high net migration rate. The U. S. consistently ranks among the top-performing economies in various global indices, including the Ease of Doing Business Index and the Global Competitiveness Report, reflecting its enduring economic strength and resilience.

In 2017, the United States boasted a labor force of approximately 160. 4 million individuals, ranking third globally behind India and China. Government employment, encompassing federal, state, and local positions, amounted to 22 million in 2010. Notably, small businesses emerged as the largest employer in the nation, employing 37% of American workers, while large businesses accounted for 36% meanwile; white-collar workers constituted 44% of the workforce as of 2022, marking a notable increase from 34% in 2000.

The private sector stands as the primary employer for 85% of working Americans, with government employment comprising 14% of the total workforce. Small businesses play a pivotal role in job creation, with over 99% of private employing organizations in the U. S. falling under this category. Remarkably, small businesses generated 64% of newly created jobs and were responsible for 70% of job creation over the past decade.

Despite fluctuations, the proportion of Americans employed by small businesses versus large businesses has remained relatively stable over the years, with some small enterprises transitioning into large corporations. However, just over half of small businesses survive beyond five years. Notably, among large businesses, several American companies rank among the world's largest employers, with Walmart leading as the largest private sector employer globally, employing 2.1 million individuals worldwide and 1.4 million in the U.S. alone.

Minority-owned businesses, representing 35% of the U.S. population, contribute significantly to the economy, with Hispanics, African Americans, Asian Americans, and Native Americans collectively owning 4.1 million businesses. These businesses generate nearly $700 billion in revenue and employ almost five million workers nationwide. The United States boasts the highest average employee income among OECD nations, with a median household income of $77,600 as of 2023.

However, certain labor-related aspects in the U.S. remain contentious. The country lacks legal guarantees for paid vacation, paid sick days, and paid family leave, setting it apart from other advanced economies. Additionally, union membership has seen a decline in recent decades, mirroring a decrease in labor's share of the economy. The World Bank ranks the United States first in the ease of hiring and firing workers, yet the nation has received criticism for its labor protections, with organizations like the International Trade Union Confederation grading it poorly. Some scholars attribute workplace-related stressors, such as toxic environments and long hours, to adverse health outcomes, suggesting that contemporary employment practices may contribute to excess deaths in the U.S.

Following the Great Recession between 2009 and 2010, the phenomenon of jobless recoveries emerged, leading to unprecedented levels of long-term unemployment. By January 2010, more than six million workers had been searching for employment for over six months, particularly impacting older workers. A year after the recession's end in June 2009, immigrants gained 656,000 jobs in the U.S., while U.S.-born workers experienced a loss of over a million jobs, partly due to demographic shifts and an aging population. In April 2010, the official unemployment rate peaked at 9.9%, with the U-6 unemployment rate (a broader measure of unemployment which includes part-time underemployed individuals) reaching 17.1%. During the period from February 2008 to

February 2010, the number of individuals working part-time due to economic reasons surged by 4.0 million to 8.8 million, representing an 83% increase in part-time workers.

By 2013, although the unemployment rate had dropped below 8%, a significant proportion of individuals remained long-term unemployed, and household income continued to decline, indicative of a sluggish job recovery. Nonetheless, the number of payroll jobs rebounded to pre-recession levels by May 2014 as the economy gradually recovered.

In comparison with the eurozone, the U. S. unemployment rate has generally remained lower since the mid-1980 s, after surpassing it in the post-war period. Over time, the composition of the workforce shifted significantly, with a growing majority employed in the services sector. Male unemployment rates consistently outpaced those of females, while unemployment rates among Caucasians tended to be lower than those among African-Americans.

Youth unemployment reached a peak of 18.5% in July 2009, marking the highest rate for that month since 1948. In May 2013, the unemployment rate among young African Americans stood at 28.2%.

The COVID-19 pandemic significantly impacted the U. S. economy, leading to a record high unemployment rate of 14.7% in April 2020. However, by June 2020, it declined to 11.1%. The pandemic-induced economic downturn resulted in a substantial contraction of Q2 GDP by 32.9% in 2020. Nevertheless, the unemployment rate experienced a rapid decline, reaching 3.9% in 2021 and further decreasing to 3.7% in May 2023.

Science and technology have played pivotal roles in the development of the United States, with notable figures and advancements shaping its trajectory. The nation's roots in the Age of Enlightenment underscored a commitment to intellectual and scientific progress, with an emphasis on reason as a guiding principle.

Reflecting this ethos, the United States Constitution empowered Congress to promote scientific and artistic innovation, laying the groundwork for systems of patents and copyrights. This framework aimed to foster creativity while ensuring eventual public access to new ideas and technologies.

### 4.3.2 U.S.-China Trade Dispute

Since January 2018, the U. S. and China have been embroiled in an economic dispute initiated by President Donald Trump. The U. S. administration imposed tariffs and other trade barriers on China, aiming to address what it deemed as China's unfair trade practices and intellectual property issues. These measures were intended to correct the U. S. –China trade deficit and to prevent forced technology transfers to China. In retaliation, China accused the Trump administration of nationalist protectionism and implemented countermeasures.

Historically, Trump was a proponent of tariffs since the 1980s, arguing that they could eliminate the U. S. trade deficit and bolster domestic manufacturing. Despite criticism from economists regarding the detrimental effects of such tariffs on the American economy, Trump's administration pursued aggressive trade policies against China.

The trade dispute intensified throughout 2019, culminating in a provisional agreement in January 2020. However, this agreement expired in December 2021, with China not meeting the expected targets for importing U. S. goods. By the end of Trump's presidency, the trade war was largely viewed as unsuccessful for the U. S. Despite this, President Joe Biden has maintained the tariffs.

Under both the Bush and Obama administrations, the U. S. had imposed trade restrictions on Chinese goods like textiles to protect domestic industries, accusing China of dumping products at below-market prices. Despite these measures, trade between the two nations grew, particularly after China joined the World Trade Organization (WTO) in 2001. The trade imbalance, however, continued to widen, driven by differing savings rates and economic policies between the two countries.

The ongoing dispute has seen various administrations criticize China's trade practices, from intellectual property issues to state-led economic strategies, which have been perceived as threats to U. S. economic supremacy. In response to these challenges, the Trump administration took significant steps, including tariff impositions and restricting Chinese investments in U. S. high-tech sectors.

China, on its part, has defended its policies, arguing against the allegations of forced intellectual property transfer and emphasizing its contributions to global technology through substantial investments in research and development. Recent developments have seen continued restrictions by the Biden administration aimed at limiting China's access to advanced U. S. technology, reflecting ongoing tensions and the complex interplay of trade, economics, and national security between the two global powers.

The trade dispute between the U. S. and China, initiated in 2018, has had far-reaching effects on both countries and the global economy. A United Nations report from November 2019 highlighted the economic damage inflicted on both nations, with increased costs for U. S. manufacturers, higher prices for consumers, and financial challenges for American farmers. In China, the tariffs have further slowed economic and industrial growth, which was already in decline.

The dispute has prompted significant shifts in global supply chains, with many U. S. companies moving their manufacturing from China to other parts of Asia. This realignment has raised concerns about an economic "decoupling" between the U. S. and China, potentially reshaping global trade relationships. While some countries have benefitted by absorbing these manufacturing shifts, others have felt the negative impacts of the trade tensions.

In response to the trade dispute, China implemented several economic measures to stabilize its economy, including increasing the personal income tax threshold and reducing value-added taxes. Despite these efforts, the country's industrial output and exports have suffered, underscoring the deep impact of the tariffs.

The effects within the U. S. have been mixed. Some industries have experienced growth, while others, especially agriculture, have suffered due to retaliatory tariffs from China. American farmers have faced severe financial challenges, leading to a decrease in agricultural exports to China and an increase in farm bankruptcies, despite federal aid.

The uncertainty and disruptions caused by the trade dispute have also led to volatility in the stock market, with significant fluctuations following tariff announcements. The ongoing dispute could influence U. S. electoral outcomes, particularly affecting regions and industries hit hardest by the tariffs.

The U. S. -China trade dispute has sparked varied reactions within China. Studies from Chinese academics acknowledge the trade dispute's economic impacts, predicting manageable but significant hits to employment and GDP.

Reactions in the U. S. are also mixed. Some Democrats criticize the trade war for burdening American consumers with higher costs, while others, including Senate Democratic leader Chuck Schumer, commend the tough stance against China's trade practices. Bipartisan support exists in some quarters of Congress, with figures like Nancy Pelosi backing Trump's tariff actions despite broader concerns about their efficacy and impact on sectors like agriculture.

American businesses have expressed significant concern over the tariffs. By 2020, over 3,500 firms sued the Trump administration, challenging the imposition of tariffs. A coalition including major retailers and manufacturers called "Tariffs Hurt the Heartland" lobbied against the tariffs, arguing they harm American consumers and businesses alike. Agricultural impacts are particularly severe, with industry representatives warning that U. S. agriculture could permanently lose market share globally.

Internationally, the trade war has not gone unnoticed. It featured on the agenda at major summits like the G20, and global leaders from the European Union to Singapore have expressed concerns about its ramifications. The EU shares some of the U. S. 's grievances against Chinese trade practices but disagrees with the method of tariffs. The trade war has slowed economic growth and investment, affecting economies worldwide. Regions like Vietnam and Malaysia have seen a boost in manufacturing due to trade diversions, but the overall global economic landscape remains fraught with uncertainty.

In summary, the U. S. -China trade dispute has elicited a wide array of responses, from domestic criticism within China to bipartisan support and concern in the U. S. , and apprehensive international reactions. The complexity of the issue reflects its global implications, touching on economic, political, and social dimensions across multiple continents. Overall, the U. S. -China trade dispute has reshaped international trade and economic policy, demonstrating the interconnected nature of global economies and the broad impacts of national decisions. With Trump's return to the White House in 2025, trade are projected to continue to influence global economic strategies and international relations.

APPLY YOUR KNOWLEDGE

1. How does the U. S. dollar's status as the world's reserve currency benefit the U. S. economy?

2. How has the U. S. managed to maintain its economic growth and resilience despite facing periodic recessions and financial crises, such as the Great Recession of 2008?

3. In what ways has the U. S. -China trade dispute reshaped global supply chains and international economic strategies, and what are the broader implications for global trade relationships and national security?

## AFTER CLASS

### KEY TERMS

Rocky Mountains
Volcanic Islands(Hawaii)
Bible Belt
Demographic Mosaic
Supreme Court
Bicameral Congress
Cold War
U. S. Constitution
Civil War
USMCA

### EXTENSION

■ Donkey vs. Elephant: The Two Major Parties in the U. S.

The political landscape of the United States has long been shaped by the rivalry between its two major parties: the Democratic Party and the Republican Party. This rivalry has profoundly influenced American politics, policy, and society over the centuries.

The origins of this rivalry date back to the early years of the republic. The Democratic Party, founded in 1828, is the oldest active political party in the United States. It emerged from the Democratic-Republican Party, which was established by Thomas Jefferson and James Madison in the 1790 s to oppose the Federalist Party. The Democratic Party initially represented agrarian interests, advocated for states'rights and limited federal government.

The Republican Party, founded in 1854, emerged as a response to the Kansas-Nebraska Act, which threatened to extend slavery into new territories. Anti-slavery activists formed the party, modernizers, and former Whigs who opposed the spread of slavery. By 1980, the Republican Party became the principal opposition to the Democrats, with its platform centered on the abolition of slavery and the promotion of economic modernization.

The Civil War(1861—1865) solidified the deep divisions between the two parties. The Republican Party, led by President Abraham Lincoln, fought to preserve the Union and end slavery. In contrast, the Democratic Party, particularly in the Southern states, was largely associated with the Confederacy and the defense of slavery. The aftermath of the Civil War and the Reconstruction era further entrenched the political rivalry, with Republicans advocating for civil rights for freed slaves and Democrats often resisting these changes.

Paty platforms and constituencies in the late 19th and early 20th centuries. The Republicans, known as the party of big business and economic progress, dominated national politics during the Gilded Age. The Democrats, on the other hand, gradually began to represent urban workers, immigrants, and Southern farmers. The New Deal era of the 1930s, under Democratic President Franklin D. Roosevelt, marked a significant realignment. The Democrats became the party of social welfare and government intervention in the economy, attracting a broad coalition of labor unions, minorities, and the working class. The Republicans, opposing the New Deal policies, began to attract business interests and advocates of limited government.

The post-World War Ⅱ era saw the continuation of this rivalry, with the Civil Rights Movement and the Vietnam War further polarizing the electorate. The Democratic Party, increasingly associated with civil rights, social progressivism, and anti-war sentiments, contrasted sharply with the Republican Party's emphasis on traditional values, strong national defense, and free-market policies. The Southern Strategy of the 1960s and 1970s, employed by Republicans, aimed to attract disaffected white Southern voters, leading to a significant shift in the political landscape.

The late 20th and early 21st centuries have been characterized by intense partisanship and ideological polarization. The Democrats, led by figures like Bill Clinton and Barack Obama, have continued to advocate for social justice, environmental protection, and healthcare reform. The Republicans, with leaders like Ronald Reagan and Donald Trump, have emphasized tax cuts, deregulation, and conservative social policies. The rivalry between the two parties has become increasingly contentious, with significant debates over issues such as healthcare, immigration, climate change, and economic inequality.

This long-standing rivalry between the Democratic and Republican parties has not only shaped the policies and governance of the United States but also reflected and influenced broader societal changes. Understanding this historical rivalry provides insight into the dynamics of American politics and the ongoing struggles over the nation's future direction.

CASE STUDY

■ The U. S. Strategy for Global Dominance

The United States has long pursued a strategy aimed at maintaining and expanding its dominance on the global stage. This strategy involves various elements, including military strength, economic influence, diplomatic efforts, and cultural presence. By examining different periods and policies, we can understand how the U. S. has sought to assert its leadership worldwide.

Historical Context

The U. S. strategy for global dominance began to take shape after World War Ⅱ. The war left the U. S. as one of the world's most powerful nations, both economically and militarily. The establishment of the United Nations and the creation of international financial institutions like the World Bank and International Monetary Fund (IMF) have helped the U. S. influence global governance.

The Cold War Era

During the Cold War (commonly 1947—1991), the U. S. focused on containing the spread of communism and countering Soviet influence. This period saw significant military build-up and numerous alliances, such as NATO, aimed at protecting Western interests. The U. S. engaged in various conflicts and interventions, like the Korean War and the Vietnam War, to prevent communist expansion.

The Marshall Plan was another key element of U. S. strategy during this time. By providing economic aid to rebuild Western European countries, the U. S. not only helped these nations recover but also ensured their alignment with Western, capitalist ideals rather than Soviet communism.

Post-Cold War to the Present

With the end of the Cold War, the U. S. emerged as the sole superpower. The 1990s saw efforts to promote demonstrated and open markets around the world. The Gulf War in 1991 demonstrated the U. S.'s military capability and willingness to use force to protect its interests and maintain global stability.

The 21st century brought new challenges and strategies. After the September 11, 2001 attacks, the U. S. launched the Global War on Terror, leading to military interventions in Afghanistan and Iraq. These actions aimed to combat terrorism and promote stability in regions considered vital to U. S. interests.

Economically, the U. S. continues to leverage its influence through institutions like the World Bank and IMF. Trade agreements, such as NAFTA and the recent USMCA, reflect efforts to maintain economic dominance and secure favorable trade conditions.

Military Presence and Alliances

A significant aspect of U. S. global dominance is its military presence. The U. S. maintains military bases around the world, enabling rapid deployment and power projection. Key alliances, including NATO, play a crucial role in extending U. S. influence and ensuring collective security.

The U. S. also invests heavily in advanced military technology and capabilities, such as aircraft carriers and stealth fighters. This technological edge is essential for maintaining its strategic advantage.

Soft Power and Cultural Influence

Beyond military and economic power, the U. S. uses soft power to maintain its global dominance. American culture, including movies, music, and fashion—has a widespread appeal and helps promote U. S. values and lifestyle. Educational exchanges and institutions, such as universities and think tanks, also contribute to this soft power by attracting international students and scholars.

Diplomatically, the U. S. engages in various international organizations and forums to shape global norms and policies. Its leadership roles in the United Nations, World Trade Organization (WTO), and other bodies are pivotal in promoting its interests and addressing global issues.

Challenges and Criticisms

Despite its dominant position, the U. S. faces significant challenges. The rise of China as a global power, along with Russia's assertiveness, presents strategic competition. Economic issues, such as trade imbalances and domestic economic challenges, also affect U. S. global influence.

Critics argue that U. S. interventions and policies sometimes lead to unintended consequences, such as regional instability or backlash against perceived American imperialism. Balancing national interests with global responsibilities remains a complex task for U. S. policymakers.

CONCLUSION

The U. S. strategy for global dominance involves a multifaceted approach, combining military strength, economic influence, diplomatic efforts, and cultural presence. By examining historical and contemporary strategies, we can understand how the U. S. has maintained its leadership role in the world. This understanding helps us analyze current geopolitical dynamics and anticipate future shifts in global power structures.

CLASS DISCUSSION

Discuss the role of international organizations, trade agreements, and cultural influence in shaping U. S. strategy. Additionally, address the challenges and criticisms faced by the U. S. in balancing these elements and the implications for its global leadership.

FOR FUN

1. Website to visit

(1) Smithsonian Magazine: Explore History, Science, Arts & Culture: engaging articles on American history, culture, science, and innovation.

(2) National Geographic: stunning photography and stories about America's landscapes, wildlife, and history.

(3) Home. Library of Congress (loc. gov): access to a vast collection of American historical documents, photos, and exhibits.

2. Video to watch

(1) Ken Burns Documentaries: Watch Ken Burns' documentaries on PBS such as "The Civil War" and "Jazz" for in-depth and visually captivating explorations of American history.

(2) Watch "America: The Story of Us" for a dramatized and comprehensive look at the key events and figures in U. S. history.

(3) Explore TED Talks for thought-provoking presentations on various topics related to U. S. history and culture.

4. Articles to read

(1) "How Has The American Dream Changed Through History?" from California Learning Resource Network

(2) "How the U. S. Became a Global Superpower?" from Everyday States.

# Unit 5 Regions as Context: Cases from the United Kingdom

> When people say England, they sometimes mean Great Britain, sometimes the United Kingdom, sometimes the British Isles, but never England.
>
> —George Mikes

## LEARNIING OUTCOMES

■ Gain a comprehensive understanding of the geographical, demographic, and cultural characteristics of Britain.

■ Identify the key features of the British parliamentary system, including the roles and interactions of the monarchy, Parliament, the Prime Minister, and other political institutions.

■ Analyze the historical and contemporary changes that have shaped British governance.

■ Describe the major economic transformations in Britain over the past 50 years, including key policies, challenges, and outcomes.

■ Explain key elements of contemporary British diplomacy, and assess the UK's strategic international relationships and policies.

## BEFORE CLASS

■ John McCormick. Contemporary Britain(Second Edition). 中国人民大学出版社,2009.

■ Speech by Rish Sunak at Conservative Party Conference 2023.
https://mp.weixin.qq.com/s/TkgcyILAW6Zc8W3LKAlKww.

After you read the above materials, please answer the following questions:

1. What is the basic situation of British geography and how about the relationship among different regions?

2. What are the main evolving periods of British history and the influences of each period?

3. What are the relationships among British political institutions and how do the political style and personal of Prime Ministers influence policies in government?

4. What are the major industries in British economy and what role does London play in the global financial system?

5. What are the relationships between the UK and the EU, the UK and the US, the UK and China?

6. What kind of political or economic orientations have been exposed in Sunak's speech?

# 5.1 Land & People

## 5.1.1 Geography

The most notable geographical facts about the UK are its small size, its status as an island state, and its moderate dimensionsin almost every way: there are no extremes in terms of distance, size, height, length, climate, or biodiversity of animal and plant life. It has no great mountain chains, rivers, estuaries, large lakes, or sweeping forests. Its highest mountain (Ben Nevis in Scotland) is less than one-sixth the height of Mt. Everest and less than one-third the height of Mont Blanc, Europe's highest mountain. Its largest lake (Lough Neagh in Northern Ireland) could fit into Lake Superior over 215 times, and its longest river (the Severn in England) is about one-twentieth the length of the Nile and one-eighth the length of the Danube, Europe's longest river. Britain has just 420 animal species and 1,600 flowering plant species, few of which are endemic to the British Isles.

Despite this, Britain is notable for its diverse landscapes, a product of geological and climatic changes over time, and centuries of human activity. Its geological history has seen it move from the southern to the northern hemisphere, with landscapes that have inclued tropical rainforests, deserts, ice caps, high mountains, and mudflats. The last significant natural influence was the Ice Age, ending 11, 700 years ago, which left Scotland slowly rising and southern England sinking, with sea levels moving up estuaries. This geological variety makes Britain, for its size, one of the richest in geological diversity worldwide.

During the Ice Age, Britain was connected to the European mainland, but rising sea levels created the island of Great Britain and its smaller neighboring islands. Britain is now separated from the continent by the North Sea and the English Channel, and from Ireland by the Irish Sea. The UK's only land border is the 488 km border with Ireland. The landscape continues to evolve today, with natural and human influences reshaping it. Physically, Britain can be divided into highland and lowland regions, with the highest lands in the southwest (Dartmoor and Exmoor), the Pennines, Wales, Northern Ireland, and Scotland, while the rest consists of plains and lowlands interspersed with moorland and gently undulating chalk downs of the southeast.

The climate of Britain is known for being moderate, with cool and wet summers and mild, largely snowless winters, although recent years have seen warmer summers. The weather, influenced by surrounding seas and air currents, is a common topic of conversation. Rainfall is well-distributed, contributing to the lush greenery characteristic of Britain. Climatologists describe it as "moderate", a polite term for the cool and wet summers and the mild and snowless winters, prompting the old joke that the only difference between the winter and the summer is that the rain is warmer in the summer. In fact, Britain—especially England—is drier than commonly perceived. This dryness, coupled with a growing population, summer time droughts, and significant leakage from the aging water distribution system, results in increasingly frequent bans on the use of hosepipes for watering gardens or washing cars. And the experience of recent years suggests that climate change is helping make British summers warmer; in both 2005 and 2006 there were long spells of hot weather with little rain, leaving large parts of Britain dry and parched. And 2006 turned out to have the highest average temperatures since records began in 1914.

The most significant influences on Britain's climate are the surrounding seas (which act as a temperature buffer that keeps coastal areas cool when inland areas are warm, and vice versa), the intersection between cool air moving down from the North Pole and warm air moving up from the tropics, and the Gulf Stream, which carries warmer water from the tropics to the Arctic, and has a moderating effect on Britain's weather, making it much warmer than areas at similar latitudes in Asia or North America. January temperatures are generally in the range of 3~5 ℃(37~41 ℉) and July temperatures are in the range of 15~25 ℃(59~77 ℉). Rainfall is usually well-distributed throughout the year and tends to be soft and steady rather than sharp and heavy, with few major storms. One of the results is the characteristic lush greenery of the British landscape, which usually lasts throughout the summer and the winter. Another result is that the British are often caught wrong-footed by more extreme weather, such as hot summers or heavy snow in winter. Whatever the conditions, weather is one of the standard topics of conversation among Britons.

### 5.1.2 People

Like many of its European neighbors, Britain is a densely populated country. In mid-2023, the population was estimated at about 67.7 million, roughly the same as France but on a land area half the size. Population density is nearly 280 people per sq km (725 per sq mile), with more than 430 people per sq km (1,000 per sq mile) in England and just 70 per sq km (180 per sq mile) in Scotland. The most densely populated areas are in and around London, Birmingham and Coventry in the Midlands, a crescent from Liverpool to Manchester and Sheffield, and clusters around Newcastle, Glasgow, Cardiff, and Belfast. The least populated regions are southwest and northern England, Wales, and most of Scotland.

England is the dominant constituent in the UK, not just by land area (53%) but also by population and demographic change. Nearly 84% of the UK population lives in England, which has seen the greatest population increase over the past century (58%, compared to just 12% in Scotland). This population is expected to continue growing, while Scotland's is already declining. Most major UK cities, including London, Birmingham, Manchester, and Liverpool, are in England, attracting people seeking jobs, wealth, and opportunity.

As in many post-industrial societies, Britain's population growth rate has been declining, currently at just 0.4% annually. The population is expected to peak around 2040 at nearly 70 million before beginning to decline. This contrasts with most other European countries, such as Germany, France, Spain, and Italy, where growth rates are smaller and populations are already declining. Migration has become a significant factor in British population changes. Natural change(the difference between births and deaths) accounted for nearly all population increases in the first half of the 20th century but fell to just 100,000~150,000 people annually by 2020. Migration shifted from a net outflow to a net inflow, reaching a record high of 606,000 in 2022.

These changes have significantly impacted Britain's diversity. Until World War Ⅱ, Britain was predominantly white, with most immigrants from continental Europe and the white dominions of the Old Commonwealth: Australia, Canada, New Zealand, and South Africa. The number of emigrants was much higher than the number of immigrants. Since 1945, particularly in the last two decades, there have been four significant developments.

1. Increasing Emigration

Emigration increased by 50% between 1994 and 2004, with 360,000 people leaving Britain in 2004. While emigrants once primarily went to the Commonweath redms and the United States, about 40% now move to other EU member states. Recent polls show more Britons considering emigration for a better quality of life, dislike of British weather, and rising living costs.

2. Immigration from the New Commonwealth

Immigration from the Indian subcontinent (India, Pakistan, Bangladesh) and the Caribbean has grown, increasing the number of non-whites in Britain from about 75~100,000(0.2% of the population) in 1945 to about 5.2 million(8.7%) today.

3. Migration within the EU

Migration to and fromother EU states has grown, with the average annual inflow of people from the EU rising from 71,000(1990) to 89,000(1990s). Recent migration flows have included work-related factors and lifestyle choices, with many Britons retiring to France, Spain, or Portugal. Workers from Eastern Europe have increased since the EU enlargement in 2004, with immigrants from the new EU member states making up about 80% of the increase in net inflows to Britain during 2003—2004.

4. Asylum Seekers

Britain's more accessible asylum policies have attracted many asylum seekers, with applications rising from 33,000 in 1992 to over 80,000 in 2002, second only to Germany in the EU. Regulations have since tightened, reducing applications to less than 30,000 annually. Most recent asylum seekers have come from the Western Balkans, Iraq, Iran, Afghanistan, Somalia, and Zimbabwe, adding to Britain's social diversity.

Britons have become increasingly mobile within the country. Once, it was typical for people to live and work in the same placefor generations. This changed with the industrial revolution, drawing people to mining towns and factories in urban centers. In recent decades, people have moved from old industrial centers in northern England, Scotland, and Wales to jobs in light industry and services in southern England and the Midlands, and from city centers to suburbs and neighboring towns, increasing the number of commuters. The biggest net movement has been out of London due to congestion, high property costs, and rising rents, although the capital's population continues to grow due to inflows from outside Britain, especially other EU states.

As in all post-industrial societies, Britain's population is aging as birth rates decline and people live longer. In 1901, over a third of Britons were under 16, and 10% were over 55; by 2024, these figures were 7% and 28%, respectively. Nearly one-quarter of adults are of pensionable age (66 for both genders), an 18% increase since 1971. This trend aligns with the rest of the EU and other industrialized countries. The aging population will have significant political and economic ramifications.

①Increased pressure on the healthcare system as more funds are needed and demand for healthcare workers grows.

②More retirees working for financial reasons are affecting workplace dynamics.

③Younger people bearing a greater social security burden as fewer working-age Britons contribute to the system while more retirees withdraw from it.

④Growing political power of the elderly due to higher voter turnout among older age groups. Concerns about the elderly's welfare have long been important, but effective lobbying by organizations representing their interests is likely to increase as the population ages.

### 5.1.3 Nationalism and Regionalism

The relationship among the four partners in the United Kingdom has often been strained due to historical subjugation by England, concerns over England's cultural, economic, and political dominance, and efforts to protect minority cultural identities. Despite being a "United" Kingdom, regionalism plays a significant role in national politics, even leading to minority support in Scotland and Wales for complete independence.

Wales lost its independence in 1282 and came under England rules between

1536—1542, leading to the development of its political institutions along English lines. Today, Wales shares the same legal and administrative systems with England. Scotland's situation was different; while the Scottish and English crowns united in 1603, political union didn't occur until 1707, and even then, Scotland retained distinct features such as different religions, legal codes, and educational structures. Ireland was partitioned in 1922, creating the Irish Free State and leaving Northern Ireland, which has been governed semi-autonomously with its own civil service, political parties, and Parliament at Stormont, except during periods of direct rule from London (1972—1999).

Differences among the Four Countries.

①Each country has its own flag, culture, writers, artists, and sports teams.

② Scotland, Wales, and Northern Ireland have regional political parties and representation in both the national British Parliament and regional assemblies.

③Class and regional differences overlap due to industrial development in the 18th and 19th centuries in Scotland, Wales, and northern England.

④Scotland and Northern Ireland have separate legal and educational systems from England and Wales, and the Church of Scotland is remains the national church from the Church of England.

⑤Wales is officially bilingual, with about 20% of the population speaking Welsh, which has had equal status with English since 1993. In contrast, only about 11. 1% of Northern Ireland's population speaks Irish Gaelic, and about 1% of Scotland's population speaks Scots Gaelic, which is near extinction.

The relationship among the four countries has fluctuated, but fears of the UK's breakup are exaggerated, as devolution (transferring selected powers from London to regional governments) since the 1960s has reduced pressures. This idea, dating back to the 1880s, gained traction in recent decades. The Conservative Party traditionally opposed devolution, fearing it could lead to full independence for Scotland. Conversely, the Labour Party, upon gaining power in 1997, quickly moved to hold referendums in Scotland and Wales, resulting in the creation of regional assemblies in 1998 and the re-establishment of Northern Ireland's assembly in 1999.

While the Scottish independence movement persists, polling data on its strength is mixed. Recent surveys show varying support, with resentment against the national government in London strongest in poorer parts of Scotland and Wales. Voter priorities are reflected in mixed support for regional political parties. In the 2003 regional assembly elections, the Scottish National Party won 23% of the vote, while Plaid Cymru won 20%. Support for both parties was lower in the 2005 general election, suggesting continued support for national parties with an undercurrent for local parties handling local issues. Improved results in the 2007 regional elections were partly due to disenchantment with Labour.

Both the UK and Ireland were part of the EU, enabling unimpeded trade between them without borders. Britain and Ireland's membership in the EU had effectively minimized the Northern Ireland issue within the framework of EU integration. However, with Britain leaving the EU, Ireland was the first to feel the impact. Post-Brexit, economic and trade exchanges between the UK and EU member states, including Ireland, faced significant challenges. This situation not only affected the UK but also dragged Ireland into economic uncertainty. The Northern Ireland issue was a crucial factor in the delays surrounding Britain's exit from the EU. In 2017, Brexit negotiations heavily focused on "the Northern Ireland border question". This issue persisted throughout subsequent negotiations. Now that Britain officially left the EU in 2020, the resolution of related follow-up problems remains to be seen.

APPLY YOUR KNOWLEDGE

1. How might the diverse cultural identities within Britain influence its political landscape and policies in the future?

2. In what ways can Britain's historical and current immigration patterns impact its social and economic development?

# 5.2 Government and Politics

## 5.2.1 The Parliamentary System

Britain is renowned as the birthplace of the parliamentary system, widely known as the Westminster model. This system, named after the area in central London where the British Houses of Parliament are situated, has been highly successful and adopted worldwide. The key elements of this system include the following.

(1) A fusion of the executive and the legislature.

(2) A symbolic head of state and a political head of government.

(3) An executive comprising a head of government and a Cabinet of ministers.

(4) Representative democracy, where elected officials are accountable to voters.

(5) Responsible government, where ministers are collectively accountable for their decisions and departmental operations.

(6) A multi-party system with strong party discipline within the legislature.

Despite Britain's long history of parliamentary governance and one of the world's oldest monarchies, its political system is dynamic and continuously evolving. Historically, changes were driven by the struggle for power between the monarchy and Parliament. In recent times, debates over the role of government, the fluctuating power balance between the Prime Minister and Parliament, and the legacy of EU membership and local governance have reshaped British politics. The administrations of Prime Ministers Margaret Thatcher and Tony Blair exemplify this evolution. Thatcher's hands-on approach and strategic exploitation of her office's implied powers, and Blair's significant institutional reforms, including changes to the House of Lords and the creation of devolved legislatures in Scotland, Wales and Nortlern Ireland, highlight these shifts.

To examine the structure of the British government and politics, we should begin with a review of constitutional principles, then look at political institutions, the Monarchy, Parliament, Political Parties and Elections, Government and the Prime Minister, the Role of the Prime Minister, the Cabinet and Ministers, the Civil Service, the Judiciary, Local Government and Devolution, the legacy of EU membership and post-Brexit adjustments, and explain their roles in the governance of Britain. By identifying the systems and institutions with the most and least influence over the political process, discussing the changes in the power balance among these institutions and examining the centralization of power in national government and the office of the Prime Minister, we can critically assess the British model of parliamentary democracy.

1. Constitutional Principles

The UK's political system operates without a single written constitution. Instead, it relies on a combination of statute law, common law, and conventions. This unique structure allows for flexibility and adaptability, reflecting the pragmatic nature of British political culture. The "unwritten" constitution is foundational, yet its lack of a single authoritative document means that conventions play a critical role in governance.

2. Political Institutions

The United Kingdom of Great Britain and Northern Ireland was formed by a series of Acts of Union, uniting the formerly distinct nations of England, Wales, Scotland, and Ireland under a single government in London. The Twenty-six countries of Ireland left the UK in 1922, becoming the Republic of Ireland, while Northern Ireland remains part of the UK.

In form, the UK is both a parliamentary democracy and a constitutional monarchy. The head of state is a king or queen, but the sovereign reigns but does not rule, meaning the monarch has formal but not real power. The country is governed in the name of the sovereign by His or Her Majesty's Government—a body of ministers from the majority party in the House of Commons who are responsible to Parliament.

3. The Monarchy

The British monarchy is the oldest secular institution in England, dating back to at least the 9th century. Initially, the monarch held significant executive powerbut always with the expectation to consult with leading men (landowning lords) for law declaration and tax collection, as established in John's Great Charter of 1215. This expectation gradually expanded to include representatives from local communities, leading to the institutionalization of Parliament in the 13th century. By the 17th century, the constitutional conflict culminated in the 1689 Bill of Rights, significantly reducing the monarch's executive authority.

The king or queen represents the unityand tradition of the nation while fulfilling certain political functions. Queen Elizabeth Ⅱ may be the best example, having ascended the throne in 1952 and reigned until her death on September 8, 2022, succeeded by her son, Charles, who became King Charles Ⅲ. She is the head of the executive, the legislature, the judiciary, and the armed forces, acting on the advice of her ministers. Her roles include formal approval of legislation, attending public events, state visits, and conferences of the Commonwealth, of which she is the head.

4. Parliament

Parliament, the supreme legislative body in the UK, consists of two houses: the House of Commons and the House of Lords. The House of Commons, with 543 elected members, holds primary legislative power. The House of Lords, comprising life peers, bishops, and hereditary peers, acts as a revising chamber, suggesting amendments to legislation proposed by the Commons. The Speaker of the House of Commons oversees debates, ensuring order and impartiality.

A Parliament term is divided into sessions, each typically lasting one year. During these sessions, Parliament debates and passes legislation, scrutinizes government policies, and represents the interests of the public. The legislative process involves multiple readings and stages of scrutiny in both houses, with the House of Commons playing the dominant role.

5. The House of Commons

The House of Commons is the primary legislative body in the UK. Its members, known as Members of Parliament (MPs), are elected in general elections. The House of Commons debates and passes laws, scrutinizes government policy, and represents the interests of the public. The Speaker of the House of Commons oversees debates and ensures that parliamentary rules are followed.

The House of Commons has the power to initiate and amend legislation, control public spending, and hold the government to account through various mechanisms, including Prime Minister's Questions and select committees.

6. The House of Lords

The House of Lords, the upper chamber of Parliament, acts as a revising chamber. It reviews and suggests amendments to legislation proposed by the House of Commons. The House of Lords consists of life peers, bishops, and hereditary peers. While it cannot block legislation indefinitely, it can delay and suggest changes to proposed laws.

Reforms to the House of Lords have been ongoing, with efforts to make it more representative and reduce the number of hereditary peers. The House of Lords Act 1999 passed by the labour government significantly reduced the number of hereditary peers, and further reforms continue to be debated.

## 5.2.2 The Governance

Britain's political landscape is dominated by two major parties: the Conservative Party and the Labour Party. The Conservative Party traditionally supports free market policies and a strong national defense, while Labour Party advocates for social equality and public ownership of key services since 2020 Labour has moderated this stance. General elections are held maximum five years, and the party that wins the majority of seats in the House of Commons forms the government.

General elections are a crucial aspect of representative democracy, allowing voters to choose their representatives in Parliament. The election campaign period witness intense political activity, with parties presenting their policies and candidates to the electorate.

1. Government and the Prime Minister

The UK government operates under a parliamentary system where the party with the majority in the House of Commons forms the government. The leader of this party becomes the Prime Minister, who appoints otherministers and leads the Cabinet. The Prime Minister represents the UK internationally and has significant influence over domestic and foreign policy. The Cabinet, consisting of senior ministers, makes decisions on government policy and is responsible to Parliament.

2. The Role of the Prime Minister

The Prime Minister is the head of government and the leader of the majority party in the House of Commons. The Prime Minister appoints Cabinet ministers, represents the UK internationally, and plays a leading role in shaping government policy. The Prime Minister's role has evolved significantly, with leaders like Margaret Thatcher and Tony Blair expanding the powers and responsibilities of the office. Thatcher's tenure saw a more centralized and decisive style of leadership, while Blair introduced significant institutional reforms, including changes to the House of Lords and the devolution to Scotland/Wales.

The Prime Minister's influence extends to all areas of government policy and administration. Regular meetings with the Cabinet and individual ministers ensure coordination and decision-making at the highest levels of government.

3. The Cabinet and Ministers

The Cabinet, composed of senior ministers chosen by the Prime Minister, is the main decision-making body of the government. It is responsible for formulating and implementing government policies. Cabinet ministers head various government departments and rely on professional civil servants. The civil service is except for special advisers rely on and remains in place regardless of changes in government, ensuring continuity and expertise in administration.

4. The Civil Service

The British civil service is a professional body of government employees who support the implementation of government policies and the administration of public services. Civil servants are non-political and remain in their positions regardless of changes in government. This continuity ensures that government functions are carried out efficiently and consistently.

Civil servants provide expert advice to ministers and play a crucial role in the development and implementation of policy. They also manage the day-to-day operations of government departments, ensuring that public services are delivered effectively.

5. The Judiciary

The judiciary in the UK is independent and operates under the principles of parliamentary supremacy and judicial review. The highest courts, known collectively as the Supreme Court, interpret laws and review the actions of government officials to ensure compliance with the law. Judges are appointed by the Crown and hold office until mandatory retirement at age 75, ensuring judicial independence.

Parliamentary supremacy means that courts cannot overrule laws passed by Parliament. However, the judiciary can interpret the meaning of statutes and review the actions of public officials to ensure they are lawful. The judiciary's role has expanded with the incorporation of European Convention on Human Rights.

6. Local Government and Devolution

Local government in the UK is responsible for a range of public services, including education, transportation, housing, and social services. Local councils are elected bodies that manage these services within their jurisdictions. The structure and powers of local government have evolved over time, reflecting the changing needs and priorities of British society.

Devolution has granted varying degrees of legislative power to regional governments in Scotland, Wales, and Northern Ireland. These devolved governments have authority over areas such as education, health, and transportation, while thecentral government retains control over defense and foreign affairs. This devolution aims to bring government closer to the people and allow regions to address their unique needs and priorities more effectively.

Devolution has introduced a new layer of complexity to British governance. In Scotland, the Scottish Parliament has substantial legislative authority, including over justice, education, and health. Wales has its own Senedd (Welsh Parliament), which has gained increased legislative powers over the years. Northern Ireland has its Assembly, which holds legislative authority over many local matters. Each of these devolved governments can tailor policies to better suit their regional needs, which reflects the evolving needs and priorities landscape of the UK.

## 5.2.3 The European Union and Brexit

The UK's relationship with the European Union has been a significant factor in its political landscape. The decision to leave the EU, known as Brexit, has had profound implications for British politics and governance. The UK continues to navigate its new relationship with the EU, balancing sovereignty with economic and political cooperation.

Brexit has led to significant changes in trade, immigration, and regulatory policies. It has also raised questions about the future of the UK itself, with renewed discussions about Scottish independence and the status of Northern Ireland. The transition period and the initial negotiations were complex, affecting various sectors of the economy and society.

The process of Brexit has highlighted the challenges of disentangling UK laws from EU regulations. It has required extensive legislative adjustments and negotiations to establish new trade agreements and regulatory standards. The long-term impact of Brexit becoming clearer, influencing the UK's economic strategies, immigration policies, and its global role.

The British political system, characterized by its long history and adaptability, continues to evolve in response to changing domestic and international contexts. Its parliamentary democracy, constitutional monarchy, and robust institutions have provided a stable framework for governance while allowing for significant reforms and adaptations. As Britain faces new challenges and opportunities, its political system remains a dynamic and integral part of its national identity. The process of governance in Britain is a testament to the nation's ability to balance tradition with innovation, ensuring that its political structures remain effective and responsive to the needs of its citizens.

APPLY YOUR KNOWLEDGE

1. How has the relationship between the monarchy and Parliament evolved over time, and what are the implications of this evolution for modern British governance?

2. In what ways has devolution transformed the political landscape of the United Kingdom, and what challenges and opportunities does it present for the future?

# 5.3 Economy

## 5.3.1 A Brief Economic History

In the 18th century, Britain emerged as a leading trading nation, establishing colonies inIndia, Asia, the Caribbean, and North America. These colonies provided raw materials for British industries, which then exported manufactured goods globally. This economic model contributed to Britain being among the first to industrialize by the 1800s, reaching peak industrial levels.

By 1900, Britain faced competition from rising powers like Germany and the United States. World WarI, World War Ⅱ, and the decolonization period in the mid-20th century further reduced Britain's economic power. After decades of decline, the economy began to recover in the 1980s.

Economic matters play a crucial role in every society, and in the last 50 years, this has been especially true for Britain. Once the world's largest economic and trading power with a strong currency, Britain faced challenges due to competition, labor union policies, and management issues. Additionally, varying government approaches to market involvement led to economic instability.

Post-World War Ⅱ, the Labour government promoted nationalization and welfare, aiding reconstruction but leading to long-term productivity and efficiency declines. By the late 1960s, Britain's economy struggled, with problems stemming from an expensive welfare system, powerful trade unions, a large public sector, and decreasing productivity and trade surpluses. The situation worsened in the 1970s, culminating in the 1978—1979 "winter of discontent", which nearly brought the economy to collapse. Media focus on economic instability influenced voters, who prioritized economic solutions.

The Thatcher government, elected in 1979, sought to reverse these trends, reducing government involvement in the market, cutting taxes, privatizing key industries, and reducing regulation. These policies, along with global economic changes, improved Britain's economic prospects by the 1990s. Wealth increased, new businesses emerged, productivity grew, and both inflation and unemployment fell. Despite cyclical concerns, Britain has become wealthier and more dynamic, although living costs have risen, primarily due to a property price boom.

Today, Britain's economy is one of the largest and most diversified globally, ranking 18th on the Human Development Index (HDI) and sixth in GDP in 2023, with a nominal GDP of £ 2,687 billion. London is a major financial center, and the country is a leading trading nation with significant natural resources, including oil, natural gas, and coal. Foreign investments have strengthened the economy, making Britain a hub for multinational mergers.

Britain excels in high-tech sectors like e-commerce and telecommunications and is home to major banking and financial firms. Agriculture, although small, remains productive, despite challenges like foot-and-mouth disease and mad-cow disease.

The industrial sector, while declining relative to other areas, remains vital. British Steel is Europe's largest steel manufacturer, and other industries include aerospace, chemicals, clothing, communications equipment, machine tools, and shipbuilding. The energy sector, contributing 10% of GDP, is highly productive, with significant coal, natural gas, and oil production.

However, in 2023, the UK had a significant current account deficit, primarily due to trade deficits. The IMF advised the government to broaden fiscal policy to promote external balance.

## 5.3.2 Economic Components

1. Manufacturing

As of 2023, manufacturing accounted for 9.7% of the UK's GDP and 8% of employment. Although the sector's importance has declined since the 1960s, it remains crucial for exports. Despite a steady increase in manufacturing output since 1945, the sector's share of employment and GDP has decreased. Heavy industries have either become more efficient or have been replaced by smaller units producing high-value goods, such as aerospace and electronics.

The largest manufacturing sector is engineering and allied industries, contributing significantly to manufacturing gross value added. Key players include global car manufacturers like BMW, Tata, and General Motors, and numerous specialist and commercial vehicle manufacturers. The aerospace and defense sectors are dominated by companies like BAE Systems, Rolls-Royce, and GKN. Other significant sectors include chemicals, pharmaceuticals, food, drink, tobacco, paper, and textiles.

2. Finance

London is a global financial hub, home to the London Stock Exchange, London Metal Exchange, and Lloyds of London. The Docklands area, developed in the 1980s, houses major financial institutions like Barclays, Citigroup, and HSBC. The City of London leads in Eurobonds, foreign exchange, energy futures, and global insurance, with over 500 banks having offices there.

The UK's financial services significantly contribute to the balance of payments, with financial exports amounting to £ 46 billion in 2023. Major cities like Leeds and Edinburgh also have substantial financial sectors.

3. Transport

The UK has an integrated transport system with extensive airports, seaports, rail, and road networks. Major airports include London Heathrow, London Gatwick, and Manchester Airport. The UK's advanced road transport system spans 396,000 kilometers, with almost 3,600 kilometers of motorways. The privatized rail network links key locations within the UK and Europe via the Eurostar connection and the Channel Tunnel. The ports and harbors industry is one of the largest in Europe, handling over 500 million tons of freight annually.

4. Energy

In 2023, the UK consumed energy equivalent to 190 million tons of oil, up from 147.3 million tons in 1990 (House of Commons Library). Transport accounted for the largest share of energy consumption at 38.83%, followed by domestic use at 28.19%, industry at 20.21%, and services/agriculture at 12.77%.

The UK was largely self-sufficient in energy until the 2000s, thanks to North Sea oil and gas and coal reserves. However, declining North Sea production and the high costs of clean coal mining means the UK is expected to become a major oil and gas importer by 2025. Concerns about an "energy gap" in generating capacity have arisen due to the expected closure of coal-fired power stations and Magnox nuclear stations by 2025.

Efforts to fill the energy gap include the construction of new gas-fired and coal-fired power stations, onshore and offshore wind farms, wave and tidal power, biogas from sewage and landfill, and biofuels. The UK has significant potential for renewable energy sources, though development has been limited.

5. Agriculture, Hunting, Forestry, and Fishing

UK agriculture is intensive and efficient, producing about 60% of food needs using less than 1.4% of the labor force (House of CommonsLibrary). The sector contributes around 0.6% of GDP, with livestock production making up two-thirds and arable crops one-third. Major crops include wheat, barley, oats, oilseed rape, maize, potatoes, and sugar beet, while livestock include cattle, chickens, and sheep. Agriculture is subsidized by the EU's Common Agricultural Policy.

The UK's fishing industry, though reduced, remains significant, with fleets based in towns such as Kingston upon Hull, Grimsby, andPeterhead. Agriculture, hunting, forestry, and fishing contributed £ 11,324 million to the UK economy in 2022.

6. Tourism

Tourism is a major industry in the UK, worth £ 120 billion to the economy in 2023, equivalent to 8.2% of GDP (House of CommonsLibrary). The sector supports 2.9 million jobs, representing 8.4% of the workforce. The UK ranked seventh in international tourism earnings in 2023, with 32.3 million overseas visitors spending £ 17.5 billion.

7. Education

Universities contribute significantly to the UK economy, generating nearly £ 62 billion annually. Higher education accounts for 2.5% of GDP, attracting international students and visitors who bring in £ 5.8 billion. The sector provides 320,000 full-time jobs, representing 1.2% of all UK jobs.

8. Property Market

The UK property market boomed until 2008, driven by economic growth, low interest rates, and property investment. The market peaked in 2004, strengthened in 2006, but began to decline in late 2007. The subsequent house price crash contributed to economic recession and increased household debt. Falling prices have made property more accessible for first-time buyers.

9. Currency

The British currency, the pound sterling, is divided into 100 pence. The Bank of England, established in 1694, serves as the central bank, executing monetary policy, issuing banknotes, and managing the national debt. The bank supports the government's goal of low inflation and oversees the financial system.

10. Taxation

UK government receipts in 2023—2024 were £ 845.6 billion, with income tax,

National Insurance contributions, and VAT as the largest sources (House of Commons Library). The tax year runs from April 6 to April 5 of the following year. The Financial Year, used for corporation tax, runs from April 1 to March 31.

11. Trade

The UK is the world's ninth-largest exporter, with principal exports including beverages, chemicals, food, fuels, and tobacco. Major export partners are the US, Germany, the Netherlands, France, Ireland, Belgium, and Spain. In 2023, the UK imported £ 726 billion worth of goods, including foodstuffs, fuels, machinery, and manufactured goods, with major suppliers being Germany, the US, China, and the Netherlands. The UK posted a £ 180 billion trade deficit for 2023, with international trade amounting to 45.2% of its GDP.

Britain's economy has undergone significant changes over the past decades. From its post-war decline to its resurgence in the 1980s under Thatcherism, and its current status as a major global financial center, the UK has continuously adapted to global economic shifts. Despite challenges, including energy security concerns and a volatile property market, the UK remains a dynamic and influential player in the global economy.

The UK's resilience and adaptability have allowed it to navigate various economic crises and transitions, positioning it as a leader in finance, high-techindustries, and global trade. The government's focus on reducing market intervention, fostering private enterprise, and integrating into the global economy has yielded positive results, contributing to economic growth and stability.

However, the country still faces ongoing challenges, such as ensuring energy security, maintaining a competitive manufacturing sector, and addressing income inequality. As the UK navigates its post-Brexit future, its ability to innovate and integrate new technologies will be crucial in maintaining its economic strength and global standing.

In conclusion, Britain's economic transformation over the past 50 years highlights the importance of adaptability and strategic policy-making in maintaining economic growth and stability. As the country continues to evolve, it must balance the need for economic competitiveness with the well-being of its population, ensuring sustainable and inclusive growth for the future.

APPLY YOUR KNOWLEDGE

1. How did the economic policies implemented by the Thatcher government in the 1980s impact Britain's long-term economic prospects, and what were some of the positive and negative consequences of these policies?

2. In the context of post-Brexit Britain, what are some potential strategies the UK could adopt to address its current account deficit and ensure sustainable economic growth?

## 5.4 International Relations in Brief

The "Special Relationship" between the UK and the US continues to be a cornerstone of Britishforeign policy. This partnership encompasses trade, defense, and intelligence sharing. In 2021, bilateral trade between the UK and the US was valued at approximately £ 196.3 billion. The two countries also collaborate closely on global security initiatives, including NATO operations, and counter-terrorism efforts. Discussions during 2023—2024 have focused on enhancing trade agreements and addressing mutual concerns such as climate change and cybersecurity. In 2023, the UK and US signed a new defense cooperation agreement aimed at enhancing joint military capabilities and interoperability.

1. UK and China

Sino-British relations are characterized by both cooperation and tension. Economically, China is a crucial trading partner, with bilateral trade reaching £ 93 billion in 2021. Chinese investments in the UK span various sectors, including real estate and technology. Likewise, the UK also has a significant investment presence in China, with numerous projects and substantial financial input.

However, political differences pose challenges. The UK's approach to China involves balancing economic interests with security and ethical considerations. In 2023, the UK government imposed stricter regulations on Chinese tech investments to safeguard national security. Additionally, the UK's engagement with the Belt and Road Initiative(BRI)-related projects reflects its strategic interest in fostering economic cooperation while navigating complex geopolitical dynamics.

2. Relations with the European Union

Post-Brexit, the UK continues to redefine its relationship with the European Union. The Trade and Cooperation Agreement (TCA) established a framework for future relations, covering trade, security, and other areas of cooperation. However, challenges remain, particularly concerning the Northern Ireland Protocol and its implications for trade between Northern Ireland and the rest of the UK.

In 2023, the UK and EU held several rounds of negotiations to address these issues, with both sides seeking to minimize disruptions and maintain a stable relationship. The UK's commitment to cooperating with the EU on shared challenges, such as climate change and global security, underscores the importance of maintaining a constructive partnership despite the complexities introduced by Brexit.

3. UK and the Commonwealth

The Commonwealth of Nations remains a significant aspect of British foreign relations, fostering cooperation and development among its 54 member states. The UK continues to play a leading role in the organization, promoting democratic values, economic development, and cultural exchange. In 2022, the Commonwealth Heads of Government Meeting (CHOGM) was held in Rwanda, where member states discussed key issues such as climate change, trade, and global health.

The UK's commitment to the Commonwealth is reflected in its foreign aid policies and investment in development projects across member states. The Commonwealth's diverse membership and shared history provides a platform for the UK to engage with a wide range of countries and address global challenges collectively.

APPLY YOUR KNOWLEDGE

1. How might the UK's focus on green economy initiatives and renewable energy investments shape its economic future and international standing?

2. What are the key challenges and opportunities presented by the UK's post-Brexit relationship with the European Union, and how might these shape the future of UK-EU cooperation?

## AFTER CLASS

### KEY TERMS

| | | |
|---|---|---|
| Nationalism | Nationalization | Monarchy |
| Devolution | Privatization | Cabinet |
| Industrial Revolution | Decolonization | Brexit |
| Westminster Model | | |

### EXTENSION

■ Offshore Balancing Strategy

Britain's offshore balancing strategy is a foreign policy approach aimed at maintaining balance in international power without extensive deployment of military forces abroad. Instead, the UK relies on a combination of diplomatic influence, alliances, and limited military presence to ensure no single power dominates key regions such as Europe, the Middle East, and Asia. This strategy allows Britain to protect its interests and maintain global stability while minimizing the costs and risks associated with large-scale military engagements.

A compelling illustration of Britain's offshore balancing strategy is the Falklands War in 1982. This conflict between Britain and Argentina over the Falkland Islands showcases how Britain used limited military force, strategic alliances, and diplomatic efforts to protect its interests.

Military Deployment

Britain swiftly deployed a naval task force to reclaim the islands, demonstrating its ability to project power without maintaining a permanent large-scale military presence in the South Atlantic.

Alliances and Diplomacy

The UK leveraged its diplomatic relationships, particularly with the United States, to garner international support and apply political pressure on Argentina.

Strategic Objective

By successfully retaking the Falklands, Britain reinforced its commitment to defending its territories and maintaining regional balance, deterring future aggression.

To better understand the strategy, the reader should consult a map online highlights key locations and movements during the Falklands War.

Key Locations: The Falkland Islands, South Georgia, and Ascension Island.

Movements: British naval task force route from the UK to the South Atlantic, highlighting the strategic deployment and supply lines.

The Falklands War exemplifies Britain's offshore balancing strategy by showcasing how the UK can effectively protect its interests through strategic deployment and alliances, without extensive permanent military presence. This approach allows Britain to influence global stability while managing resources efficiently.

CLASS DISCUSSION

According to the above introduction of Britain's offshore balancing strategy, search more information and discuss how this strategy has been applied to the European continent?

■ Anglo-Saxonism

Anglo-Saxonism refers to a cultural and ideological concept that emphasizes the historical, cultural, and racial heritage of the Anglo-Saxon people, particularly those of England. This ideology often highlights the perceived superiority of Anglo-Saxon institutions, legal systems, and cultural traits, and has played a significant role in the national identity of countries like the United Kingdom and the United States.

Solo Work: Do more research on Anglo-Saxonism to understand its historical roots, ideological elements, influence on national identity, etc., and then, draw a flowchart and give examples, illustrating the spread and influence of Anglo-Saxonism.

CASE STUDY

■ Winston Churchill

Sir Winston Churchill was born on November 30, 1874, coming from a prominent family—his father, Lord Randolph Churchill, was a leading Conservative politician. He served in the British Army, working as a war correspondent before entering politics.

Churchill held various governmental positions throughout his career, including First Lord of the Admiralty, Minister of Munitions, Chancellor of the Exchequer, and Home Secretary. He was a member of both the Conservative and Liberal parties at different points in his career.

Churchill is most famous for his leadership as Prime Minister during World War Ⅱ. He took office in 1940, after the resignation of Neville Chamberlain. His resolute stance against Nazi Germany and his inspirational speeches rallied British morale during the darkest days of the war. Notable speeches include "We shall fight on the beaches", "Their finest hour", and "Never was so much owed by so many to so few". Churchill served as Prime Minister again from 1951 to 1955, focusing on domestic policies and international relations during the early Cold War period. He received the Nobel Prize in Literature in 1953 for his historical writings.

Churchill's legacy is complex; he is celebrated for his wartime leadership and oratory skills, which were pivotal in securing Allied victory in Word war Ⅱ. However, he also had controversial views and policies, including his stance on the British Empire and issues such as the Bengal Famine of 1943. Churchill is often seen as embodying the spirit of British resilience and determination, particularly during crises. His ability to articulate the collective will and determination of the British people made him a unifying figure during Word war Ⅱ.

CLASS DISCUSSION

What kind of influence has Churchill left on British politics? What makes him a cultural icon in British and global culture? How can we comment on his historical position?

FOR FUN

1. Websites to visit

(1) British Museum. https://www.britishmuseum.org/

(2) UK travel and heritage-Britain Express UK travelguide. https://www.britainexpress.com/index.htm

2. Movie to see

*Brave Heart* (1995)

The movieis a 1995 epic historical drama film directed by and starring Mel Gibson. It is a fictionalized account of the life of William Wallace, a 13th-century Scottish warrior who led the Scots in the First War of Scottish Independence against King Edward I of England.

3. Article to read

张健,《英国脱欧的战略影响》

张健,中国现代国际关系研究院欧洲所所长、研究员,主要从事欧洲一体化、欧盟外交及中欧关系、欧美关系等问题研究。

# Unit 6 Regions in Global Context: The Unification of Europe

> Europe will not be made all at once, or according to a single plan. It will be built through concrete achievements which first create a de facto solidarity.
>
> —Jean Monnet

## LEARNIING OUTCOMES

■ Gain a comprehensive understanding of the historical evolution and ideological foundations of European integration.

■ Evaluate the specific economic impacts of European integration on member states, including the benefits and drawbacks of the single market and common currency.

■ Investigate the social and cultural impacts of European integration, focusing on fostering a sense of European identity and promoting cultural diversity.

■ Critically assess the political structures and power relations within the EU, including the roles and functions of the European Commission, European Parliament, and European Council.

■ Explore the global influence of a unified Europe, focusing on its role in international organizations, diplomatic strategies, and impact on global governance.

## BEFORE CLASS

■ Srdjan Cvijic, Marie Jelenka Kirchner, Iskra Kirova, Zoran Nechev. "*From Enlargement to the Unification of Europe: Why the European Union Needs a Directorate General Europe for Future Members and Association Countries*". https://www.opensocietyfoundations.org/publications/from-enlargement-to-the-unification-of-europe

After you read the above materials, please answer the following questions.

1. How do the authors describe the shortcomings of the current European Commission

structures?

2. Why do the authors believe there is a need to create a dedicated directorate general to handle the affairs of future member and association countries?

3. What are the main challenges faced by the Western Balkans, Georgia, Moldova, and Ukraine mentioned in the book?

4. What role will the new Directorate General Europe play in advancing the accession process for these countries?

5. What specific reform suggestions are proposed in the book to improve the efficiency of the European Commission?

6. What impact will these suggestions have on the future of the European Union if implemented?

# 6.1 The History of Europe

## 6.1.1 Expansion and Competing Interests of European Powers

In the late 19th and early 20th centuries, a significant phenomenon in international relations was that most countries worldwide were directly or indirectly controlled by the major European powers, stretching from the Atlantic Ocean in the west to the Ural Mountains in the east. To monopolize investment areas, markets for goods, and sources of raw materials—as well as topreemptively seize strategic and military points of interest—major powers such as Britain, France, Russia, and Germany were in a state of high tension, with the specter of war looming. The competition for overseas colonies directly exacerbated existing conflicts among these great powers, setting Europe on the path to war.

In the 19th century, Britain leveraged its strong economy, powerful navy, and extensive overseas colonies to become the "Empire on which the sun never sets". The opening of the Suez Canal in 1869 marked a significant point, as the maritime route through the Mediterranean, Suez Canal, Red Sea, and Indian Ocean was deemed the lifeline to Britain's Asian colonies. Following the 19th-century shift from an agricultural to an industrial economy, a substantial portion of Britain's food and industrial raw materials came from colonies such as India and Australia. Simultaneously, its manufactured goods needed to be shipped to overseas markets, making the security of maritime routes and the establishment of strategic bases and supply stations along these routes a primary concern for the British Empire. Additionally, to invest the substantial capital accumulated during the Second Industrial Revolution in underdeveloped regions, London's financial institutions began heavily investing in railway and road construction, port improvement, and other projects to ensure smooth investment channels. To protect its overseas interests, the British Empire engaged in various diplomatic maneuvers and local military conflicts with other great powers in the Near East, Central Asia, North Africa, and the Far East before World War Ⅰ.

After being supplanted by Germany and losing its status as a dominant continental power in 1871, France concentrated its diplomacy on the threat posed by Germany. Constraining and guarding against Germany became the core of French foreign policy under successive leaders. In the 1870s and 1880s, due to Bismarck's skilled and intricate diplomatic efforts, France failed to find a stable and reliable ally in Europe. By the early 1890s, after forming a military alliance with Russia, France's policy towards Germany became more proactive and aggressive. This period saw French colonial policy influenced by Framce's stance against Germany. In the latter half of the 19th century, France actively pursued colonial expansion, particularly during Bismarck's administration, as Germany encouraged French imperialism to divert its focus from European affairs. By the early 20th century, France had become the world's second-largest colonial empire, controlling vast territories, including approximately one-third of the African continent, French Indochina in Southeast Asia, and several island chains in the South Pacific. Compared to Britain, France's economic development was less dependent on foreign trade and did not require grain imports. Additionally, French financial capital was not invested in colonies to the extent seen with British capital. The French government viewed foreign investment as a diplomatic tool, actively encouraging private capital to enter developing Eastern Europe. Through investments in Russia, the Austro-Hungarian Empire, the Ottoman Empire, and the newly formed states on the Balkan Peninsula, France aimed to create a network of countries reliant on French financial support, thereby encircling Germany and enhancing its diplomatic influence.

World War Ⅰ profoundly altered the old international relations system. Four empires—the German Empire, the Russian Empire, the Austro-Hungarian Empire, and the Ottoman Empire—collapsed. The establishment of the world's first socialist regime,

Soviet Russia, marked the emergence of a new form of state and ideology. Several new republics emerged in Europe, including Germany, Austria, Poland, Czechoslovakia, Latvia, Lithuania, Estonia, and Finland, fundamentally changing the political map of Europe. In terms of international relations, the pre-war struggle among the six powers (Britain, France, the United States, Russia, Germany, and Japan) was transformed. With Russia withdrawing due to revolution and Germany defeated, the contest now involved the former Entente Powers and the rising influence of the United States and Japan. Japan, though relatively weak, leveraged its geographical advantages to seek dominance in East Asia and the Pacific, while the United States, with its strength, confidence, and idealism, began to replace European hegemony.

After World War Ⅱ, Western Europe completely lost its centuries-long central role in international relations. Countries like the UK, France, Germany, and Italy had to rely on U. S. economic aid to stabilize their political order. In the bipolar U. S. -Soviet confrontation, unity became the most prudent choice for Western European countries to maintain their own security and interests. Simultaneously, the post-war scientific and technological advances, further internationalization of production and capital, and increased economic interdependence laid the economic foundation for European unification. Similar historical backgrounds and political systems provided the social foundation for Western European integration.

## 6.1.2 The European Integration Movement

In September 1946, Churchill delivered a speech in Zurich advocating for the establishment of a "United States of Europe", urging France and Germany to set aside past grievances and become partners. However, the UK's ultimate aim was not to join the European integration but to establish a relationship with it similar to that of the U. S., thereby reviving the glory of the British Empire. The United States, aiming to use Western Europe to contain the Soviet Union, also strongly promoted European integration. Although France initially aimed to weaken Germany, it adjusted its policy under U. S. pressure, seeking to restrain Germany through alliances. Germany actively supported European unification, viewing it as an opportunity to overcome the aftermath of its defeat and rejoin the international community.

Franco-German reconciliation was crucial for European unification. On May 9,

1950, French Foreign Minister Schuman proposed the establishment of the "European Coal and Steel Community" (ECSC), known as the Schuman Plan. He advocated integrating the coal and steel industries of France and West Germany with those of other Western European countries under a supranational authority. Following negotiations, France, West Germany, Italy, Belgium, the Netherlands, and Luxembourg signed the Treaty of Paris on April 18, 1951, establishing the ECSC. The success of the ECSC spurred further European unification. On March 25, 1957, the six countries signed the Treaties of Rome, establishing the European Economic Community (EEC) and the European Atomic Energy Community (Euratom). The treaties aimed to remove customs barriers between member states, to eliminate obstacles to the free movement of persons, services, and capital, to implement common economic policies, and set up institutions like the European Investment Bank and the European Social Fund to enhance employment opportunities and living standards.

The establishment of the EEC significantly boosted the foreign trade and economic development of its member states and laid the groundwork for further European integration. As Western European economies recovered and grew, the EEC sought to break free from U. S. control and pursue an independent foreign policy, becoming an influential third force outside the U. S. -Soviet rivalry.

In 1958, Charles de Gaulle came to power in France, advocating for an independent foreign policy and becoming a representative of Western European resistance against U. S. control. He shifted from the post-war policy of dismantling and weakening Germany, promoting Franco-German cooperation to escape U. S. control and establish France as a major power. West German Chancellor Adenauer, wary of the U. S. compromising German interests with the Soviet Union, also sought Franco-German cooperation to improve Germany's international image. Their mutual interests led to closer ties, culminating in the signing of the Élysée Treaty in January 1963, marking the reconciliation and furthering the independence of Western Europe.

While promoting Franco-German cooperation, de Gaulle aimed to establish an independent nuclear defense system for European unification. Nuclear weapons symbolized great power status. Although part of NATO, France sought equal standing with the U. S. and the UK. Skeptical of the U. S. 's commitment to protecting Western Europe, de Gaulle pursued an independent nuclear force, freeing France from NATO's military integration. In 1958, de Gaulle demanded equal status in NATO and access to its leadership, but the U. S. and the UK refused. By 1966, France then withdrew its navy from NATO command, expelled U. S. troops from France, and rejected U. S. nuclear weapons and bombers on French soil. By 1960, France successfully tested its atomic bomb, breaking the U. S. nuclear monopoly in Western Europe.

France's independent actions alarmed the U. S., prompting Kennedy to propose a Multilateral Nuclear Force (MLF) plan to integrate French nuclear forces under U. S. control. De Gaulle rejected the MLF and the Partial Test Ban Treaty signed by the U. S., the UK, and the Soviet Union in 1963. France withdrew from NATO's integrated military command in 1966, expelling U. S. forces from French soil. De Gaulle aimed to play a third force between the U. S. and the Soviet Union, supporting détente, understanding, and cooperation with the USSR. He shared with the Soviets the goals of restraining Germany and diminishing U. S. influence in Europe. In March 1960, during Khrushchev's visit to France, de Gaulle proposed a détente policy with the Soviet Union and envisioned a Europe "from the Atlantic to the Urals". His visit to the USSR in 1966 marked the shift in Western Europe's approach from confrontation to dialogue with the Soviet Union and Eastern Europe.

## 6.1.3 Theories of Integration

How to avoid war between nation-states is the central question of the first theory. Federalist and functionalist theories proposed the containment of the nation-state, while transactionalism sought to theorize the conditions for the stability of the nation-state system.

One of the most influential theories of European integration is neo-functionalism, developed by Ernst B. Haas (1958) and further studied by Leon Lindbergh (1963). This theory focuses on the spillover effect of integration, which leads to more integration. By contrast, another influential theory in integration studies—liberal intergovernmentalism—focuses on the pursuit of national preferences through bargaining. This theory was developed by Andrew Moravcsik in the 1990s, building on the "intergovernmentalism" theory of Stanley Hoffmann and others. It's still very influential. The important debate between neo-functionalism and liberal intergovernmentalism remains central to understanding the developments and setbacks of European integration.

As the empirical world has changed, so has the theory and understanding of

European integration. Today, there is a relatively new focus on complex policy making and multi-level governance (MLG) within the EU that attempts to produce a theory of the functioning and development of the EU.

According to a 2016 study, European integration deepened through a process of "failed progress", in which intergovernmental negotiations led to incompleteness because they force countries with different preferences to reach the lowest common denominator solution. Incompleteness unleashes the forces that lead to crisis. In response, member states once again agreed to adopt the lowest common denominator solution to resolve the crisis and deepen integration. So far, this continuous cycle of incremental reform, policy failure, and further reform has succeeded in sustaining European integration and the euro.

## 6.1.4 Expansion of European Integration

In the 1960s, the UK's economic growthlagged behind the EEC. Remaining outside the EEC threatened its global and Commonwealth political influence. The U. S. also supported the UK's EEC membership to conterbalance European autonomy. In August 1961, the Macmillan government formally applied to join the EEC. On January 1, 1973, after a long wait, the UK, along with Denmark and Ireland, acceded to the EEC members.

European integration accelerated in the 1980s. Greece joined the EEC in 1981, followed by Spain and Portugal in 1986, expanding the EEC to 12 members. Alongside expansion, internal integration deepened. The 1984 Fontainebleau Summit resolved the EEC budget issue and established a "Special Committee" of national leaders to draft a European Union plan. The 1985 Milan Summit reached consensus on establishing a unified internal market and developing advanced technology but sparked intense debates on political cooperation.

A united Europe strengthened its position. In the 1970s, European integration made it a key player in the global economy and an essential force in political dynamics. Western Europe sought new international roles, maintaining its U. S. alliance while expanding relations with the Soviet Union and the Third World, seeking broader global influence in the 1970s and 1980s.

APPLY YOUR KNOWLEDGE

1. How did the competition for overseas colonies among major European powers in the late 19th and early 20th centuries exacerbate existing conflicts and set the stage for World War Ⅰ?

2. How did the concept of European integration evolve in the post-World War Ⅱ period, particularly with initiatives like the Schuman Plan, and what role did Franco-German reconciliation play in this process?

# 6.2 Europe in the Age of Globalization

## 6.2.1 The Birth and Development of the European Union

The establishment of the European Union (EU) is a significant achievement in the movement toward European integration. On December 10, 1991, at the 46th summit of the European Community in Maastricht, the Netherlands, the Treaty on European Economic and Monetary Union and the Treaty on Political Union were initialed, collectively known as the Maastricht Treaty. The main contents of this treaty include three aspects, which also constitute the three pillars of the EU.

①Establishing an Economic and Monetary Union, with a schedule for creating a European Central Bank and implementing a single currency.

② Elevating the political cooperation mechanism in diplomatic affairs among member states to a Common Foreign and Security Policy (CFSP), which, for certain decisions, allows for specific majority voting instead of requiring unanimous consent for each decision.

③Establishing a cooperation mechanism among member states in judicial and civil affairs.

The Maastricht Treaty represents a breakthrough in the European integration process, indicating that the European Community would develop into a union with economic, political, diplomatic, and security functions. Therefore, the Maastricht Treaty is considered a milestone in the process of European integration. The treaty came into effect on November 1, 1993, officially marking the birth of the European Union (EU).

European economic integration also made significant progress. On January 1, 1994, the European Economic Area (EEA) was established, consisting of the 12 EU countries and five European Free Trade Association countries (Austria, Finland, Sweden, Norway, and Iceland). This area, with a population of 372 million and accouned for more than 40% of the world's trade, aimed to create a unified large market for the free movement of goods, people, services, and capital between EU and non-EU countries, thereby promoting economic development and integration among its members. On July 1, 1998, the European Central Bank (ECB) was formally established, tasked with "maintaining monetary stability", managing key interest rates, reserves, currency issuance, and formulating European monetary policy. The ECB was created to facilitate the circulation of the euro and is a product of European economic integration. On January 1, 1999, the euro was officially introduced. Most EU member states joined the Eurozone, except for countries such as the UK and Denmark, which opted out due to national interests.

The EU also accelerated its expansion, admitting new members in several rounds. In January 1995, Sweden, Finland, and Austria became among the first new members after the establishment of the EU. To accommodate the eastward expansion of the EU and promote deeper integration, the EU summit in Nice in December 2000 adopted the draft Treaty of Nice. This treaty addressed internal institutional reforms and issues arising from expansion, such as the composition of the European Commission, allocation of commissioner seats, effective majority voting mechanisms, and the number of seats in the European Parliament after enlargement. After a series of preparations and a long wait by applicant countries, the EU experienced its largest expansion on May 1, 2004, with 10 Central and Eastern European and Baltic countries joining. Romania and Bulgaria officially became EU members on January 1, 2007, followed by Croatia on July 1, 2013. The EU thus expanded to 28 member countries, with a population of 500 million and an area of 4.325 million square kilometers, formed a supranational group.

In tandem with its expansion, the EU also undertook significant institutional reforms. Initially, the European Council operated on a rotating presidency system, with each country holding the presidency for six months. The head of state or government of the rotating presidency country would serve as the European Council's rotating president. The Lisbon Treaty, which came into effect on December 1, 2009, brought about major changes in the EU's organizational structure and operational mechanisms in three main areas.

①Replacing the rotating presidency system with a permanent President of the European Council, seen as the "President of the European Council", who represents the EU on the international stage with a term of two and a half years, renewable once.

②Merging the roles of the High Representative for Foreign Affairs and Security Policy of the European Council and the Commissioner for External Relations of the European Commission into a new High Representative of the Union for Foreign Affairs and Security Policy, similar to a foreign minister role, responsible for the EU's external policy with expanded powers, including control over external aid funds.

③Transferring some policy areas that previously required unanimous consent to majority voting to avoid a single country's veto blocking policies, thereby improving the efficiency of the EU's operational mechanisms.

In 2009, Belgian Prime Minister Herman Van Rompuy was elected as the first "EU President", and EU Trade Commissioner Catherine Ashton from the UK was appointed as the "EU Foreign Minister". This resolved the longstanding issue of the U. S. not knowing whom to call when seeking to communicate with Europe, as remarked upon in the 1970s. The EU has since become the region with the highest level of regional integration in the world today.

### 6.2.2 The Common Foreign and Security Policy of the EU

The EU's Common Foreign and Security Policy (CFSP) originated from Western Europe's cooperation in diplomacy and security during the Cold War and is one of the three main pillars of the EU, aimed at "speaking with one voice".

The end of the Cold War changed the international security environment, fundamentally altering the nature of European security. The confrontation with the Soviet bloc gave way to diffuse security challenges such as regional conflicts, terrorism, nuclear proliferation, and environmental crises. The rapid reunification of East and West Germany alsoposed significant pressure and challenges to other EC member states, particularly France, highlighting the need to restrain Germany once again. These changes made it necessary and feasible for EC countries to enhance cooperation in diplomacy and security. In response to this backdrop, the Maastricht Treaty proposed the establishment of a Common Foreign and Security Policy.

The preamble of the Maastricht Treaty stated that EU member states were resolved to implement a common foreign and security policy, including the eventual framing of a common defense policy, which might in time lead to a common defense, to enhance Europe's unity and independence and promote peace, security, and progress in Europe and the world. The first significant test for the EU after its establishment was the Bosnia-Herzegovina conflict. Despite proposing various peace plans, the EU was unable to implement them. To enhance its security and defense capabilities, the Amsterdam Treaty signed on October 2, 1997, emphasized the EU's responsibilities and status in CFSP, further clarifying its security and defense goals and stipulating EU reliance on the Western European Union for humanitarian, rescue, peacekeeping, and crisis management tasks.

The Kosovo War exposed Europe's "limited capabilities" and the imbalance of power between Europe and the U. S., directly prompting the development of the EU's common defense policy. The EU summit in Cologne, Germany, in June 1999 adopted a declaration on strengthening the European Security and Defense Policy (ESDP), deciding to incorporate the Western European Union into the EU as its defense pillar, thus providing Europe with a reliable military force. The summit also appointed the first High Representative for CFSP, giving the EU an official spokesperson for foreign affairs. These measures marked a decisive step forward in the EU's CFSP. Subsequently, the EU accelerated its efforts to advance common defense. At the Helsinki summit in December 1999, the EU approved the European Security and Defense Plan, aiming to establish a rapid reaction force of 50,000 ~ 60,000 troops by 2003, capable of being deployed within 60 days and maintaining operations for at least one year, enabling the EU to make decisions and take effective military action in regional crises without NATO involvement. To this end, the EU also decided to establish a permanent Political and Security Committee, a Military Committee composed of defense ministers and chiefs of staff from member states, and a Military Staff to coordinate European defense decision-making. The Nice summit in 2000 approved the European Security and Defense Policy report, clarifying the cooperative yet independent relationship between the European rapid reaction force and NATO. In November 2003, the EU decided to establish the European Defense Agency to strengthen its defense capabilities in crisis resolution, coordinating member states' defense resources and arms production. The Lisbon Treaty, which came into effect at the end of 2009, introduced a series of significant reforms in the CFSP field, clarifying the legal status and operational objectives of various institutions and making numerous institutional innovations.

However, since diplomacy and security involve sensitive national sovereignty issues, sovereign states, especially major powers, are reluctant to relinquish their independence in these areas. Additionally, European defense has traditionally been dominated by NATO, led by the U. S., which constrains the implementation of the EU's CFSP. The EU's diplomatic differences were starkly exposed during the Iraq War, with France and Germany opposing the U. S. invasion while countries like Poland actively supported the U. S., leading to former U. S. Defense Secretary Donald Rumsfeld's remark that Europe had split into "new Europe" and "old Europe". On November 13, 2017, foreign and defense ministers from 25 EU countries signed a landmark joint defense agreement in Brussels—the Permanent Structured Cooperation (PESCO) defense agreement. According to the agreement, the EU should establish a defense coordination mechanism, set up a defense coordination command body, and form military action entities, including personnel, weapons, logistics, and a common EU military hospital, all within the framework of the EU defense cooperation agreement. This marked a significant steptowards the EU's independence and strengthening of its common security and defense policy.

### 6.2.3 Challenges Facing the European Union

As integration deepens, the EU has been vigorously promoting common foreign policy and engaging in multilateral diplomacy, aiming to play a more significant role on the international stage. The EU's foreign policy targets can be divided into three major regions: the first region comprises the EU member states; the second region includes neighboring countries such as those in the Middle East, North Africa, and the Eastern Partenship countries; and the third region encompasses distant countries and regions. In global affairs, the EU has established regular summit meeting mechanisms with major powers like the United States and China and has close cooperative relationships with international organizations such as the United Nations and NATO. The EU has played a crucial role in preventing conflicts in Eastern European countries with territorial and ethnic disputes, facilitating their smooth political and economic transitions. It has also actively participated in mediating international disputes and has focused on global issues such as the environment, non-proliferation, humanitarian aid, and human rights.

However, it must be acknowledged that the EU, as a unique international actor, does not fully possess the status and will of a sovereign state. With varying interests and policy positions among its member states, the EU struggles to unify foreign strategies and policy measures, which affects its ability to exert greater influence on the international stage. In recent years, the EU has faced severe challenges such as the debt crisis, refugee crisis, and Brexit.

The financial crisis that originated in the United States in 2008 affected many EU member states, leading to a serious "European debt crisis". In December 2009, the three major global rating agencies downgraded Greece's sovereign rating, exacerbating the Greek debt crisis and triggering the European debt crisis. The debt crisis subsequently spread to Ireland, Portugal, Spain, and Italy. According to Eurostat, in 2009, the overall fiscal deficit of the Eurozone accounted for 6.3% of GDP, and government debt accounted for 78.7% of GDP, both exceeding the EU limits of 3% and 60%, respectively. Due to the high level of interdependence within the EU, there were concerns that the debt crisis would affect the entire EU, and some even questioned the European integration model, leading to the emergence of so-called "Eurosceptics". It should be noted that while the debt crisis was influenced by the U.S. subprime mortgage crisis, it was primarily due to the various institutional defects within the European integration itself. Addressing these defects will be a pressing task for the EU in the future.

In 2015, Europe experienced the largest refugee crisis since World War Ⅱ, which tested both Europe's capabilities and its traditional values, as well as the Common Foreign and Security Policy (CFSP). A large number of refugees from war-torn and poverty-stricken regions in Syria, Afghanistan, Iraq, and Africa took risks to reach geographically close and affluent the Europe. According to the United Nations High Commissioner for Refugees (UNHCR), the number of refugees arriving in Europe by sea increased from 216,054 in 2014 to 1,015,078 in 2015, an increase of nearly 370%. Furthermore, more than 3,500 refugees drowned or went missing each year in 2014 and 2015, with the number reaching 5,096 in 2016. On April 14, 2015, a smuggling ship from Libya to Italy capsized, resulting in the deaths of about 400 people. On September 3, 2015, European newspapers published the image of a drowned 3-year-old Syrian refugee, Aylan, on a Turkish beach, bringing global attention to the humanitarian crisis of the refugee problem in Europe and leading to criticism of European refugee policies. In response to the influx of refugees, the EU implemented measures such as member states sharing refugee quotas, supporting neighboring countries in controlling refugee flows, and expanding refugee reception centers. However, due to various factors, these measures were not effectively implemented. The influx of refugees dealt a severe blow to Europe's already struggling economy and strained public facilities and welfare system, leading to strong protests from citizens in many countries. Anti-refugee conflicts erupted in Denmark and Sweden. The presence of terrorists among the refugees was associated with an increase in terrorist attacks in Europe, adding domestic pressure on governments to accept refugees and causing significant divisions within the EU over refugee policies.

In addition to the debt crisis and refugee crisis, Brexit dealt another major blow to the process of European integration. On June 23, 2016, the UK held a referendum on "Brexit", with 52% of voters supporting leaving the EU and 48% supporting remaining. After 43 years of integration into Europe, the UK once again chose "splendid isolation", marking a significant reversal in the process of European integration. Post-Brexit, the EU faces the challenge of dealing with Eurosceptic factions within its member states and strengthening cohesion. Whether Brexit will be an opportunity for the EU to further strengthen internal integration or the beginning of its disintegration remains to be seen.

Under the multiple shocks of the debt crisis, terrorism, and refugee crisis, far-right populist parties have risen in many major EU member states (such as France, Italy, Germany, and Austria). In France, the far-right National Front led by Marine Le Pen gained significant influence, receiving the highest number of votes in the first round of the 2015 regional elections. In Italy, the Eurosceptic Five Star Movement became the third-largest party in parliament in the 2013 elections and won significant victories in Rome and Turin in the 2016 local elections, challenging the ruling Democratic Party led by Prime Minister Matteo Renzi. In Germany, the far-right Alternative for Germany entered the Berlin state parliament for the first time in September 2016, with its support reaching new highs following the Berlin Christmas market terrorist attack in December 2016. In Austria, the far-right Freedom Party candidate Norbert Hofer nearly won the second round of the presidential election in December 2016. Far-right parties in the Netherlands, Belgium, Denmark, Sweden, Greece, Hungary, and Slovakia are also altering traditional political landscapes to varying degrees. The increase in parliamentary seats and influence of these parties poses new challenges to European integration. If the EU cannot overcome the numerous problems and crises it currently faces, a divided Europe is not an impossibility.

APPLY YOUR KNOWLEDGE

1. How did the Maastricht Treaty of 1991 contribute to the economic and political integration of Europe, and what were the key components that laid the foundation for the European Union?

2. What impact did the enlargement of the European Union in the 2000s have on the political and economic landscape of Europe, particularly with the inclusion of Eastern European and Baltic countries?

## 6.3 Cooperation and Competition in China-EU Relations

1. Economic and Trade Cooperation

Economic and trade cooperation remains the cornerstone of China-EU relations. Despite the pandemic's impact, China became the EU's largest trading partner in 2020, with total trade in goods reaching € 586 billion. The conclusion of negotiations on the Comprehensive Agreement on Investment (CAI) in December 2020 is a significant milestone in China-EU economic relations. The CAI aims to provide better market access, ensure a level playing field, and enhance investment protection for both parties, promoting mutual investment and economic growth. In the post-pandemic era, China and the EU will continue to deepen economic and trade cooperation in various sectors, such as green and digital economies. The EU's Green Deal and China's commitment to carbon neutrality by 2060 provide opportunities for cooperation in renewable energy, energy efficiency, and sustainable development. The digital economy, including 5G, artificial intelligence, and e-commerce, also offers potential for collaboration, leveraging both parties'technological advancements and market potential.

2. Strategic Competition and Systemic Rivalry

Despite the positive aspects of economic cooperation, China-EU relations are also marked by strategic competition and systemic rivalry. The EU views China as a "systemic rival" in promoting alternative models of governance and economic development. Issues such as market access barriers, intellectual property protection, and state subsidies remain contentious points in bilateral economic relations. The EU's emphasis on values-based diplomacy and its efforts to promote international norms and standards often clash over China's approach to governance and development. This systemic rivalry will continue to shape China-EU relations, influencing policy decisions and diplomatic interactions.

3. Multilateralism and Global Governance

China and the EU share a common interest in promoting multilateralism and strengthening global governance. Both parties support a rules-based international order and the role of multilateral institutions such as the United Nations (UN), World Trade Organization (WTO), and World Health Organization (WHO). In the post-pandemic era, China and the EU will collaborate on global issues such as climate change, public health, and sustainable development, contributing to global stability and prosperity. The EU's commitment to multilateralism aligns with China's advocacy for a "community with a Shared Future for mankind". However, differences in approaches and priorities may lead to friction in multilateral forums. China's approach to global governance, which emphasizes sovereignty and non-interference, reflects its commitment to respecting the unique paths and choices of different nations. While the EU and China may have different perspectives on issues such as human rights, democracy, and the rule of law, these differences can be seen as opportunities for dialogue and mutual learning. Both sides can work together to find common ground and contribute to a more inclusive and diverse global governance framework, recognizing the value of each other's contribution and experiences.

4. Policy Recommendations for China-EU Relations

To navigate the complexities of China-EU relations in the post-pandemic era, the following policy recommendations are proposed.

①Enhancing Strategic Dialogue and Mutual Trust: Strengthening strategic dialogue at all levels, including high-level political dialogues, sectoral dialogues, and people-to-people exchanges, is essential for building mutual trust and understanding. Both parties should enhance communication and coordination on strategic issues, including regional security, economic policies, and global governance.

②Promoting Win-Win Economic Cooperation: China and the EU should focus on win-win economic cooperation, leveraging their respective strengths and complementarities. Advancing the ratification process of the CAI and addressing market access barriers, intellectual property protection, and fair competition will foster a conducive environment for mutual investment and trade. Cooperation in green and digital economies should be prioritized, aligning with the global transition to sustainability and digitalization.

③Addressing Systemic Rivalry through Dialogue and Engagement: While systemic rivalry may persist, China and the EU should manage their differences through dialogue and engagement. Constructive engagement on human rights, labor standards, and environmental sustainability can contribute to mutual understanding and cooperation. Both parties should seek common ground and practical solutions to address contentious issues, avoiding escalation and confrontation.

④Strengthening Multilateralism and Global Governance: China and the EU should enhance their cooperation in multilateral institutions and promote a rules-based international order. Joint efforts on global issues such as climate change, public health, and sustainable development can contribute to global stability and prosperity. Both parties should advocate for reforming and strengthening multilateralinstitutions to better address global challenges and reflect the changing dynamics of the international system.

⑤Promoting People-to-People Exchanges and Cultural Understanding: Enhancing people-to-people exchanges and cultural understanding is crucial for fostering mutual trust and friendship between China and the EU. Academic exchanges, cultural programs, and tourism can facilitate dialogue and cooperation at the societal level, contributing to a positive and constructive bilateral relationship.

In the post-pandemic era, China-EU relations will be characterized by both cooperation and competition. Economic and trade cooperation will remain the cornerstone of bilateral relations, while strategic competition and systemic rivalry will shape policy decisions and diplomatic interactions. By enhancing strategic dialogue, promoting win-win economic cooperation, addressing systemic rivalry through engagement, strengthening multilateralism, and promoting people-to-people exchanges, China and the EU can navigate the complexities of their relationship and contribute to global stability and prosperity.

APPLY YOUR KNOWLEDGE

1. What economic and social challenges does the EU face in the post-pandemic era?

2. How might the implementation of the Comprehensive Agreement on Investment (CAI) influence the economic and trade relationship between China and the EU, particularly in the sectors of green and digital economies?

## AFTER CLASS

### KEY TERMS

Colonial expansion
Strategic base
Diplomatic maneuver
Alliance system
Debt crisis
Refugee crisis
Security system
Fiscal integration
European integration
European Central Bank(ECB)
European Economic Area(EEA)

### EXTENSION

■ EU Efforts in Coordinated Global Development

The European Union has been actively engaged in global efforts to address major challenges and promote coordinated development. These efforts span across various critical areas, including climate change, Refugee and Immigration Policy, advanced technology and innovation, and international trade and economic cooperation.

1. Climate Change

The EU has committed to ambitious climate targets, including reducing greenhouse gas emissions by at least 60% by 2030 compared to 1990 levels, and achieving climate neutrality by 2050.

Initiatives such as the European Green Deal aim to transform the EU into a modern, resource-efficient, and competitive competitiveness.

The EU Emissions Trading System (ETS) is one of the world's largest carbon markets, incentivizing reductions in greenhouse gas emissions.

2. Refugee and Immigration Policies

The EU has developed a Common European Asylum System to ensure fair and efficient asylum procedures.

Policies and programs like the EU-Turkey Action Plan aim to manage migration flows and support refugees.

The EU supports integration programs to help immigrants and refugees settle and contribute to their new communities.

3. Advanced Technology and Innovation

Horizon Europe is the EU's key funding program for research and innovation, with a budget of € 100.2 billion for the period 2021—2027.

The EU aims to become a global leader in digital technology and has launched initiatives such as the Digital Europe Programme.

The investment in AI, cybersecurity, and advanced manufacturing technologies positions the EU at the forefront of technological innovation.

4. International Trade and Economic Cooperation

The EU is one of the world's largest trading blocs and has signed numerous free trade agreements with countries and regions around the world.

Initiatives like the EU-Japan Economic Partnership Agreement and the Comprehensive Economic and Trade Agreement (CETA) with Canada promote open and fair trade.

The EU supports Sustainable Development Goals (SDGs) and collaborates with international organizations to promote economic growth and reduce poverty globally.

## CLASS DISCUSSION

According to the above introduction of the EU's efforts in coordinated global development, search for more information and discuss how these efforts have impacted global politics and economics.

## CASE STUDY

### ■ Jean Monnet

1. Background

Jean Monnet was born on November 9, 1888, in Cognac, France, into a family of cognac merchants. His early exposure to international trade and finance deeply influenced his views on economic cooperation and integration.

Monnet did not attend university but started working in the family business andtraveled extensively, gaining a wealth of practical experience in international affairs. His career as an international civil servant began during World War Ⅰ when he served as a French government representative to coordinate supplies with the British government.

2. Contributions to European Integration

Jean Monnet is widely regarded as one of the founding fathers of the European Union. His vision and efforts were pivotal in laying the groundwork for European integration.

(1) Schuman Plan and European Coal and Steel Community (ECSC)

In 1950, Monnet, along with French Foreign Minister Robert Schuman, proposed the Schuman Plan, which aimed to pool French and German coal and steel production under a single, supranational authority. This proposal led to the creation of the ECSC in 1951, marking the first step towards European integration.

(2) High Authority of the ECSC

Monnet became the first President of the High Authority of the ECSC, the executive body responsible for managing the coal and steel industries of member states. Under his leadership, the ECSC fostered economic cooperation and reduced the potential for conflict between France and Germany.

(3) Treaty of Rome

Monnet's influence extended to the signing of the Treaty of Rome in 1957, which established the European Economic Community (EEC) and the European Atomic Energy Community (EURATOM). These treaties laid the foundation for the modern European Union.

(4) Action Committee for the United States of Europe

In 1956, Monnet founded the Action Committee for the United States of Europe, which played a crucial role in advocating for further integration and the creation of a common market.

3. Legacy and Influence

Jean Monnet's vision of a united Europe was driven by his belief that economic integration would lead to lasting peace and prosperity. His pragmatic approach to supranational governance helped transform Europe from a continent marked by frequent wars into a region characterized by cooperation and stability.

Monnet's legacy is evident in the structures and institutions of the European Union today. His ideas on economic integration, shared sovereignty, and supranational governance continue to influence EU policies and frameworks.

CLASS DISCUSSION

1. What kind of influence has Jean Monnet left on European integration?

2. What are the key principles and ideas Monnet advocated for that continue to shape the EU today?

3. How can we comment on his historical position and his vision for a united Europe?

FOR FUN

1. Video to watch

Rise of Empires: Ottoman (2022)

In this programme, we follow the camera through time and space to the glory of the Ottoman Empire. It uses unique perspectives and narrative techniques to show the rise, expansion and decline of the Ottoman Empire, making people feel like they are in the magnificent river of history.

2. Article to read

贺之杲. 欧洲一体化研究：西方叙事与中国视角

贺之杲，中国社科院欧洲研究所助理研究员、副研究员，主要研究领域是欧洲政治与国际关系、中欧关系、地区一体化组织

# Unit 7 Regions in Global Context: Oceans and Technology

Control of the sea by maritime commerce and naval supremacy means predominant influence in the world.

—Alfred Thayer Mahan

The sea, once it casts its spell, holds one in its net of wonder forever.

—Jacques Cousteau

## LEARNING OUTCOMES

■ Identify the four oceans and major seas in the world, where they are located, and what are the major countries on their shores.

■ Explain the strategic significance of oceans and seas for countries in the world.

■ Identify the major international organizations around the oceans and seas, and their major members.

■ Explain the most influential international conventions related to oceans and seas.

■ Identify as many technologies for exploring, controlling and utilizing the sea as possible, and their future prospects.

## BEFORE CLASS

■ Resource 1 The Ocean's Importance—7 Reasons why you should care about it—Oceanpreneur (theoceanpreneur.com)

■ Resource 2 古代海洋文化及其现代意义

■ Resource 3 Ancient Mariners of the Mediterranean (nationalgeographic.org)

After you read the above materials, please answer the following questions.

1. How do you describe the importance of the ocean?

2. What is the traditional value of ancient China towards seas?

3. What are the features of the Mediterranean civilizations?

4. Why China didn't become a marine power before the Opium War?

## 7.1 International Organizations around Oceans and Seas

International organizations related to the world's oceans and seas span a broad spectrum of focus areas, including political, military, economic, and environmental aspects. These organizations play pivotal roles in fostering cooperation, ensuring security, promoting sustainable economic growth, and protecting marine environments across the globe.

1. International Maritime Organization (IMO)

The International Maritime Organization (IMO), also known in French as Organisation maritime internationale and in Spanish as Organización Marítima Internacional, is a specialized agency of the United Nations tasked with regulating maritime transport. The IMO was formed following a United Nations conference in Geneva in 1948 and officially began operations a decade later with its first meeting on March 17, 1958. Based in London, United Kingdom, as of 2024, the IMO comprises 176 Member States and three Associate Members.

The main function of the IMO is to establish and uphold a comprehensive regulatory framework for shipping, covering areas such as maritime safety, environmental protection, legal issues, technical cooperation, maritime security, and the efficiency of shipping. The organization is governed by an assembly that convenes biennially. Administrative and financial matters are managed by a council of 40 members elected from the assembly. The IMO operates through seven main committees aided by several technical subcommittees. It also allows other UN agencies to observe its proceedings, and qualified non-governmental organizations can be granted observer status.

The IMO's ongoing operations are supported by a permanent secretariat, staffed with representatives from member countries. The secretariat is led by a Secretary-General, who is elected periodically by the assembly, and includes various divisions dedicated to marine safety, environmental protection, and conference management.

2. NATO(North Atlantic Treaty Organization)

NATO(North Atlantic Treaty Organization) is an international military alliance formed by 33 member states from Europe and North America. The organization was established on April 4, 1949, with the signing of the North Atlantic Treaty. A central tenet of the treaty, outlined in Article 5, commits member countries to consider an armed attack against any one member as an attack against them all, obligating mutual defense including the use of armed forces if necessary. However, Article 6 restricts this mutual defense to attacks occurring in specific geographic locations, including the North American and European mainlands, islands north of the Tropic of Cancer, the entire region of Turkey, and initially French Algeria, though the latter's applicability ceased in July 1962. Notably, territories such as Hawaii, Puerto Rico, French Guiana, the Falkland Islands, Ceuta, or Melilla do not fall under Article 5's umbrella.

The membership of NATO is predominantly European, with 30 European countries and two North American countries. The alliance has seen several rounds of expansion, especially after the end of the Cold War. Between 1994 and 1997, NATO established wider forums for regional cooperation, including the Partnership for Peace, the Mediterranean Dialogue initiative, and the Euro-Atlantic Partnership Council. These initiatives aimed to foster closer relations between NATO and neighboring countries.

While all member states have militaries, Iceland is an exception, as it does not have a traditional army but maintains a coast guard and a small unit of civilian specialists for NATO operations. Among its members, three countries—France, the United Kingdom, and the United States—are recognized nuclear weapons states. Originally founded by 12 countries, NATO has expanded to include additional members, with the latest additions bringing its membership to 32 by 2024.

NATO continues to look toward future expansion under its "Open Doors" policy and currently recognizes Bosnia and Herzegovina, Georgia, and Ukraine as aspiring members, reflecting its ongoing strategic interests and commitment to collective security in the Euro-Atlantic area.

3. The Asia-Pacific Economic Cooperation(APEC)

The Asia-Pacific Economic Cooperation(APEC) is an inter-governmental forum that includes 21 member economies from the Pacific Rim. Established in 1989 and headquartered in Singapore, APEC promotes free trade and economic integration throughout the Asia-Pacific region. The initiative was started following the success of ASEAN's post-ministerial conferences in the mid-1980s, aiming to foster ties between Asia-Pacific economies and open up new markets for agricultural products and raw materials outside of Europe.

APEC is recognized as one of the premier multilateral blocs and one of the oldest forums in the region, exercising substantial influence. The forum holds an annual APEC Economic Leaders'Meeting, attended by the heads of government from all member economies. These meetings are hosted on a rotating basis by the member economies and are known for a tradition where leaders wear the national costume of the host country, though observance varies.

APEC also includes three official observers: the Association of Southeast Asian Nations (ASEAN) Secretariat, the Pacific Economic Cooperation Council, and the Pacific Islands Forum Secretariat. Additionally, the host economy for each year is generally invited to participate in the G20 meetings, emphasizing APEC's role in both regional and global economic contexts.

4. The Indian Ocean Rim Association (IORA)

The Indian Ocean Rim Association (IORA) is an international organization that brings together 23 countries bordering the Indian Ocean. Founded initially as the Indian Ocean Rim Initiative in Mauritius in March 1995, IORA was officially established with the signing of the Charter of the Indian Ocean Rim Association for Regional Cooperation in March 1997. The formation of IORA was conceived during a visit by former South African Foreign Minister Pik Botha to India in November 1993 and was further advanced by Nelson Mandela's presidential visit to India in January 1995. South Africa, India, Mauritius, and Australia were the core initiators, with seven other nations joining at the formal launch: Indonesia, Sri Lanka, Malaysia, Yemen, Tanzania, Madagascar, and Mozambique.

IORA operates as a tripartite forum that includes representatives from government, business, and academia, aimed at promoting cooperation and facilitating economic and social development within the region. Key areas of focus include trade facilitation, investment promotion, and regional social advancement. The organization's coordinating secretariat is based in Ebene, Mauritius.

IORA's governance structure features several integral bodies, including the Council of (Foreign) Ministers (COM), which is the apex body. This council's meetings are preceded by gatherings of various sub-groups: the Indian Ocean Rim Academic Group (IORAG),

Indian Ocean Rim Business Forum (IORBF), Working Group on Trade and Investment (WGTI), and the Committee of Senior Officials (CSO). These groups collectively work to deepen integration and cooperation among member states across multiple levels of interaction.

5. The Arctic Council

The Arctic Council is a prominent intergovernmental forum dedicated to addressing issues relevant to the Arctic governments and the indigenous peoples of the region. It includes eight member states with territories in the Arctic Circle: Canada, Denmark, Finland, Iceland, Norway, Russia, Sweden, and the United States. Additionally, other countries and organizations can participate as observer states and indigenous permanent participants, respectively.

The foundation for the Arctic Council was laid in 1991 with the signing of the Arctic Environmental Protection Strategy by the eight Arctic countries. This strategy was a precursor to the formal establishment of the Arctic Council, which was officially formed with the Ottawa Declaration in 1996. The Council was created to foster cooperation, coordination, and interaction among the Arctic states, including significant involvement from Arctic Indigenous communities, with a focus on sustainable development and environmental protection.

The Council has been actively involved in research and discussions on pivotal issues like climate change, oil and gas development, and Arctic shipping. In 2011, it achieved a significant milestone by concluding the Arctic Search and Rescue Agreement, marking the first binding treaty under its framework, which aimed to enhance cooperative search and rescue operations in the Arctic.

Overall, the Arctic Council remains a crucial platform for addressing and managing the complexities and challenges of the Arctic environment, balancing national interests with sustainable development and the well-being of indigenous populations.

6. The Association of Southeast Asian Nations (ASEAN)

The Association of Southeast Asian Nations (ASEAN) is a significant political and economic alliance consisting of 10 Southeast Asian countries. It represents a combined population of over 600 million people and covers a land area of 4.5 million $km^2$. In 2022, ASEAN's collective GDP, measured at purchasing power parity (PPP), was approximately US $ 10.2 trillion, accounting for about 6.5% of the global GDP. The member states are known for being among the fastest-growing economies globally.

ASEAN was established with the primary aims of accelerating economic growth, social progress, and cultural development within the region. It also seeks to promote regional peace and stability based on justice, the rule of law, and adherence to the principles of the United Nations Charter. Over time, ASEAN has expanded its goals to include the establishment of a shared security regime, somewhat mirroring the European Union.

ASEAN is a key player in international diplomacy, engaging with other major supranational entities and global organizations. It is considered a major partner of the United Nations and interacts with other regional groups like the SCO, PA, GCC, MERCOSUR, CELAC, and ECO. ASEAN hosts diplomatic missions worldwide, enhancing its network of global relationships. Its influential role in regional and global affairs has positioned it as a central forum for cooperation in the Asia-Pacific region.

ASEAN's success has significantly influenced the formation and operation of some of the largest trade blocs in history, such as APEC and the Regional Comprehensive Economic Partnership (RCEP). These engagements underscore ASEAN's role as a global powerhouse in shaping economic and trade policies beyond its regional boundaries.

Overall, ASEAN continues to be a crucial driver of regional integration and cooperation in Southeast Asia, impacting broader economic and geopolitical dynamics in the Asia-Pacific and beyond.

7. The Caribbean Community

The Caribbean Community (CARICOM or CC) is an intergovernmental organization that functions as a political and economic union. It includes 15 member states—14 nation-states and one dependency—and five associate members spread across the Americas and the Atlantic Ocean. Established in 1973 when its four founding members signed the Treaty of Chaguaramas, CARICOM's primary goal is to foster economic integration and cooperation among its members, ensuring equitable sharing of the benefits of integration, and coordinate foreign policy.

The main activities of CARICOM are the following.

(1) Coordinating economic policies and development strategies.

(2) Creating special projects for less-developed countries within its jurisdiction.

(3) Operating as a regional single market for many of its members, known as the Caricom Single Market.

(4) Resolving regional trade disputes.

The secretariat of CARICOM is based in Georgetown, Guyana, and the organization holds official observer status at the United Nations General Assembly.

Originally formed by English-speaking Caribbean countries, CARICOM now includes all independent Anglophone island countries, Belize, Guyana, Montserrat, and Suriname, as well as all other British Caribbean territories and Bermuda as associate members. English was the sole working language until the 1990s. The organization became multilingual with the addition of Dutch and Sranan Tongo-speaking Suriname in 1995 and French and Haitian Creole-speaking Haiti in 2002. Spanish was introduced as the fourth official language in 2003. In July 2012, CARICOM considered making French and Dutch official languages. A significant development occurred in 2001 with the signing of a revised Treaty of Chaguaramas that facilitated the transition from a common market to the CARICOM Single Market and Economy (CSME), which also led to the establishment of the Caribbean Court of Justice.

8. The Organization of the Black Sea Economic Cooperation (BSEC)

The Organization of the Black Sea Economic Cooperation (BSEC) is an international, regional organization aimed at fostering political and economic initiatives to boost cooperation, peace, stability, and prosperity within the Black Sea region. Officially established in 1992 through the Summit Declaration and the "Bosphorus Statement" signed in Istanbul by leaders from eleven countries, including Turkey's President Turgut Özal, BSEC set up its headquarters, known as BSEC PERMIS, in Istanbul in 1994. The organization became a full-fledged regional economic entity in 1999 when its charter came into effect, marking the formal acknowledgment of its international legal status.

Over the years, BSEC has expanded, with Serbia joining in 2004 and North Macedonia in 2020, bringing the membership count to thirteen. The organization primarily focuses on enhancing the development of small and medium-sized enterprises (SMEs) and entrepreneurship in its member countries through various workshops and initiatives in collaboration with entities like the Konrad Adenauer Foundation and ERENET.

BSEC includes both nations that border the Black Sea and others without direct access. Its current members consist of Albania, Armenia, Azerbaijan, Bulgaria, Georgia, Greece, Moldova, Romania, Russia, Turkey, Ukraine, North Macedonia, and Serbia. Despite not all members having a Black Sea coastline, they are connected either through strategic geographical links like rivers or political and economic interests. Notably, North Macedonia's admission followed a period of vetoes and geopolitical tensions involving

Greece and Turkey concerning membership decisions. Additionally, BSEC also hosts observer states from various regions, expanding its influence and interactions globally.

9. The Pacific Islands Forum (PIF)

The Pacific Islands Forum (PIF) is a pivotal inter-governmental organization that fosters cooperation among the countries and territories across Oceania. Founded in 1971 as the South Pacific Forum, it was renamed in 1999 to the Pacific Islands Forum to better reflect its comprehensive Oceania-spanning membership that includes northern and southern Pacific island countries, along with Australia. The Forum holds observer status at the United Nations General Assembly.

The primary mission of the PIF is to enhance the economic and social well-being of the people in the South Pacific by promoting cooperation between governments and international agencies, and advocating for the interests of its members. The Forum's activities and decisions are facilitated by the Pacific Islands Forum Secretariat, which evolved from the South Pacific Bureau for Economic Co-operation. The Secretariat also undertakes various technical programs in areas such as economic development, transport, and trade, and plays a crucial role in harmonizing regional positions on diverse political and policy issues.

Australia and New Zealand, as the larger and more affluent members, play significant roles within the Forum, providing aid and serving as major export markets for the other island countries. They have also been involved in regional peacekeeping and stabilization operations, such as those in the Solomon Islands starting in 2003 and Nauru from 2004 until its withdrawl in 2009, under the auspices of the Forum and guided by the Biketawa Declaration of 2000. Despite these cooperative endeavors, the Forum has seen some challenges, notably with Palau and other countries like the Federated States of Micronesia, Kiribati, and Nauru announced intentions to leave the Forum in 2021 due to disputes over leadership elections. However, departures were paused in 2022 pending reforms, and Kiribati has recently expressed intentions to rejoin, indicating ongoing efforts toward reconciliation and unity within the organization.

APPLY YOUR KNOWLEDGE

1. In the context of global ocean governance, what role do international organizations play in addressing issues like marine pollution, overfishing, and climate change, and how can their effectiveness be enhanced through improved cooperation

and policy implementation?

2. What are the specific sustainable development goals related to oceans and seas?

## 7.2 United Nations Convention on the Law of the Sea

The United Nations Convention on the Law of the Sea(UNCLOS), also known as the Law of the Sea Convention/Treaty, is an international treaty that sets a comprehensive legal framework for all marine and maritime activities. As of May 2023, it has been ratified by 168 countries and the European Union.

The convention emerged from the third United Nations Conference on the Law of the Sea(UNCLOS Ⅲ), held from 1973 to 1982, replacing the earlier 1958 Convention on the High Seas treaties. It officially came into effect in 1994, following Guyana's ratification, which marked the 60th country to do so. In 2023, the convention had been expanded to include a High Seas Treaty, enhancing protection for marine life ininternational waters through measures such as Marine Protected Areas and environmental impact assessments.

Although the United Nations Secretary-General handles ratification and accession instruments and the UN supports the convention's meetings, the UN Secretariat itself does not have a direct role in implementing the convention. Instead, implementation involves various bodies including the International Maritime Organization, the International Whaling Commission, and the International Seabed Authority (ISA), the latter of which was specifically established by UNCLOS.

The United Nations Convention on the Law of the Sea (UNCLOS) modernized the traditional "freedom of the seas" principle, which from the 17th century limited national rights to a narrow 3-nautical-mile zone off a nation's coast, based on the range of cannon fire. Beyond this zone, the seas were considered international waters, open to all but owned by none.

By the mid-20th century, nations began extending their territorial claims to better control natural resources, enforce pollution controls, and protect fisheries. Notably, in 1945, President Harry S. Truman declared U.S. jurisdiction over all natural resources on its continental shelf. Following this, several other countries, including Chile, Peru, and Ecuador, expanded their maritime jurisdiction to 200 nautical miles to encompass lucrative fishing grounds.

By 1967, the trend had shifted significantly from the traditional 3-mile limit, with most nations adopting a 12-mile territorial limit, and a few extending up to 200 miles. Today, the 3–mile limit is rarely used, with notable exceptions including certain areas of Australia, Belize, Japan, Papua New Guinea, and some British Overseas Territories like Gibraltar.

UNCLOS, which came into force in 1994, does not address territorial disputes or sovereignty issues, which are governed by customary international law. Additionally, UNCLOS supports the United Nations Sustainable Development Goal 14, aiming for the conservation and sustainable use of oceans and marine resources.

In 1958, the United Nations hosted its first Conference on the Law of the Sea (UNCLOS Ⅰ) in Geneva, Switzerland, leading to the creation of four treaties.

(1) Convention on the Territorial Sea and Contiguous Zone, effective from September 10, 1964.

(2) Convention on the Continental Shelf, effective from June 10, 1964.

(3) Convention on the High Seas, effective from September 30, 1962.

(4) Convention on Fishing and Conservation of Living Resources of the High Seas, effective from March 20, 1966.

While UNCLOS Ⅰ achieved significant outcomes, it did not resolve the issue of the breadth of territorial waters.

The second conference, UNCLOS Ⅱ, took place in 1960 but failed to produce any new agreements. The conference largely saw developing nations participateted without a significant voice, often aligned with either the United States or the Soviet Union.

The third United Nations Convention on the Law of the Sea (UNCLOS) established a comprehensive legal framework for managing marine resources and maritime activities, replacing the fragmented older laws. The convention, which resulted from discussions that started in 1973 and concluded in 1982, was ratified by the 60th state, Guyana, in 1993 and came into force in 1994.

UNCLOS defines various maritime zones.

(1) Internal Waters: Inside the baseline, where a coastal state has full control.

(2) Territorial Sea: Up to 12 nautical miles from the baseline, where the coastal state has sovereignty but must allow "innocent passage".

(3) Contiguous Zone: Up to 24 nautical miles from the baseline, where the state can

enforce laws on customs, immigration, and pollution control.

(4) Exclusive Economic Zones (EEZs): Extends 200 nautical miles from the baseline, within which a state has sovereign rights to to explore/exploit natural resources.

(5) Continental Shelf: Extends to the natural prolongation of the land territory to the outer edge of the continental margin, up to 200 nautical miles or more, subject to specific limits on resources of the seabed.

The convention also allows for "innocent passage" through territorial seas and sets out rights for archipelagic states by allowing them to draw baselines around the outermost points of the outermost islands. Navigation, overflight, and the laying of submarine cables and pipelines are permitted in the EEZ.

Moreover, UNCLOS introduces a legal framework for deep seabed mining beyond national jurisdictions, managed by the International Seabed Authority, and emphasizes the protection of the marine environment and the promotion of marine scientific research.

Landlocked nations are afforded rights of access to and from the sea, ensuring freedom of transit through neighboring states. This comprehensive framework has significantly structured maritime boundaries and resource management, aiming to maintain peace and order in the world's oceans.

The principles and regulations established by the UNCLOS and related international agreements are actively applied in various maritime scenarios worldwide. For instance, territorial waters and the right of innocent passage often come under scrutiny in international incidents, such as the capture of the USS Pueblo by North Korea in 1968, where North Korea claimed the U. S. Navy vessel had entered its territorial waters, a claim disputed by the U. S. asserting it was navigating in international waters. Similarly, nations routinely exercise their rights to navigate through other states'territorial waters under innocent passage, avoiding internal waters and without posing threats.

Exclusive Economic Zones (EEZs) are another focal point of international maritime law, countries like Norway and Canada manage fish stocks within their EEZs using quotas and sustainable practices to ensure conservation of marine resources, aligning with UNCLOS guidelines.

On the continental shelf, countries exploit resources within and below the seabed, such as Norway's development of oil and gas fields in the North Sea, operating under rights granted by the UNCLOS. High seas freedoms also play a crucial role in global maritime operations, evident in anti-piracy operations off Somalia's coast by international naval forces and the laying and repair of undersea cables by telecommunications companies, both protected by UNCLOS.

Deep seabed mining, particularly in areas beyond national jurisdictions like the Clarion-Clipperton Zone, is managed by the International Seabed Authority (ISA), which grants exploration licenses to various countries and private enterprises. Maritime safety and environmental protection are also key aspects of international maritime law, with regulations enforced through inspections by entities like the U. S. Coast Guard to ensure compliance with MARPOL regulations and the application of the International Regulations for Preventing Collisions at Sea (COLREGs) in incidents such as the 2017 collision between the USS Fitzgerald and MV ACX Crystal.

These instances underscore the extensive application of maritime laws and conventions in managing international waters, resolving disputes, and ensuring sustainable utilization of marine resources, highlighting the ongoing relevance and necessity of UNCLOS and its associated frameworks in governing maritime interactions.

APPLY YOUR KNOWLEDGE

1. How does UNCLOS address the balance between coastal states' sovereignty and the rights of other states to navigate and utilize the oceans, particularly in areas such as the exclusive economic zones and the high seas?

2. Can you explain the concept of the Exclusive Economic Zone (EEZ) under UNCLOS?

## 7. 3 Ocean Technology

Ocean technology includes a vast array of disciplines and equipment that play critical roles in exploring, utilizing, and protecting the world's oceans. This field includes naval architecture, marine navigation, underwater acoustics, and an array of marine technology, each contributing to the safety, efficiency, and sustainability of marine operations.

## 7.3.1 Naval Architecture

Naval architecture, or naval engineering, is a branch of engineering that combines mechanical, electrical, electronic, software, and safety engineering to designing, building, maintaining, and operating ships and marine structures. It's a field that requires knowledge of both basic and advanced research, design, and development. Naval architects are involved in everything from the initial design to the final construction of a vessel, including its trials, operation, maintenance, launching, and dry-docking when necessary.

This field covers several areas, starting with hydrostatics, which is concerned with how ships behave when at rest in water. This includes calculating how buoyant a vessel is, its weight in the water, and its stability—important for ensuring it can return to an upright position if tilted by waves, wind, or changes in load. Hydrodynamics, another area, focuses on how water flows around the ship's hull and parts like propellers or rudders. This is key for understanding how ships move through water, including how they are powered and controlled.

The structural aspect of naval architecture deals with choosing the right materials and analyzing the overall strength and durability of the ship. Ships are typically constructed with steel, and their designs include carefully planned panels that form the hull, deck, and walls, ensuring the ship can withstand various stresses while at sea.

Ship design also involves planning the layout and features of a ship, such as safety systems, space allocation, and fire protection. Construction methods depend on the materials used; for example, steel ships are built by welding cut and bent steel plates according to precise designs.

Over the years, naval architecture has moved from being more of a traditional craft to a science, thanks to advancements in computer technology and software. These tools help naval architects more accurately predict and improve ship performance across various conditions. They handle everything from stability tests to resistance and propulsion analysis, helping ensure the ship operates safely and efficiently.

Naval architects are central to this complex process, coordinating with specialists in various fields to meet the challenges of marine design and construction. They work in diverse environments such as shipyards, design offices, and regulatory agencies, applying their deep understanding of engineering principles to create ships that are safe, efficient, and environmentally friendly. Their work is crucial not just in building new ships but also in ensuring existing ones are suitably updated and maintained.

Naval architecture has witnessed numerous groundbreaking achievements that have significantly shaped the design, construction, and operation of ships and marine structures. From the transformational shift from wooden to iron and steel ships in the19th century, naval architecture began its journey toward modernization. This change, exemplified by the launch of the SS Great Britain in 1843, the first iron steamer to cross the Atlantic, offered enhanced strength, size, and resistance to elements compared to wooden ships.

The advancement continued with the replacement of sail power with steam engines, marking another revolution in the 19th century. Steam engines provided reliability and speed irrespective of wind conditions, transforming naval strategy and boosting maritime commerce. Later, the introduction of turbine engines in the early 20th century further increased efficiency, benefiting vessels like the RMS Queen Mary by enhancing their operational capabilities.

World War Ⅱ spurred innovations such as modular construction techniques, which involved the use of prefabricated sections allowing for quicker and more efficient shipbuilding. This method was vital for mass-producing vessels like Liberty ships, which were crucial to the war effort. The post-war era saw the adoption of Computer-Aided Design (CAD) in naval architecture, revolutionizing the design process with precise simulations and testing before construction, thus improving safety, efficiency, and cost-effectiveness.

Materials technology also advanced with the use of composites and reinforced plastics, which allowed for the construction of lighter, stronger vessels better suited for combating combat the harsh marine environment. These materials have proved particularly beneficial in building high-speed boats and specialized vessels such as submarines and icebreakers.

The 1960s brought about dynamic positioning systems, enabling vessels to maintain their position through their own propellers and thrusters, critical for the operations like deep-sea oil drilling and sensitive maritime research. Additionally, the field saw significant strides in ship safety and stability with the development of features like the bulbous bow, anti-rolling tanks, and advanced stability software. These innovations have helped ships reduce resistance, enhance fuel efficiency, and maintain stability in adverse sea conditions.

In response to growing environmental concerns, naval architects have increasingly focused on designing greener ships. Innovations such as LNG-powered engines, solar-powered systems, and sophisticated waste management solutions have started to minimize the environmental impact of maritime operations.

Moreover, the legacy of the Titanic tragedy in 1912 led to pivotal changes in ship safety standards, including improved lifeboat capacities, enhanced hull and compartment designs, and better ice detection systems. These developments have had a lasting impact on modern safety regulations in maritime design.

These milestones not only demonstrate the dynamic and evolving nature of naval architecture but also its profound impact on global trade, military strategy, and marine conservation, driven by continuous technological advancements, safety needs, and environmental considerations.

## 7.3.2 Oil Exploitation

An oil platform, also known as an oil rig or offshore platform, is a large structure with facilities designed to extract and process petroleum and natural gas lying beneath the seabed. These platforms often include accommodations for workers, although it's common for a separate accommodation platform to be connected by a bridge to the production platform. Oil platforms are mostly found on the continental shelf, but they can also operate in lakes, inshore waters, and inland seas. The platform might be fixed to the ocean floor, made as an artificial island, or designed to float.

Oil platforms house various types of facilities for offshore drilling operations, including bottom-founded drilling rigs like jackup barges, combined drilling and production facilities, and mobile offshore drilling units such as semi-submersibles and drillships are capable of operating in water depths up to 3,000 meters. In deeper waters, these structures are held in position by dynamic positioning systems rather than fixed anchoring.

The history of offshore drilling dates back to the late 19th century, starting with submerged oil wells in fresh water and later in salt water. Over the years, significant developments have included the construction of the first mobile steel barges for drilling in the brackish coastal areas of the Gulf of Mexico in the early 1930s, and the introduction of fixed platforms, compliant towers, and the first semi-submersible in the mid-20th century. Innovations like the floating production, storage, and offloading

(FPSO) facilities have also been pivotal in advancing offshore drilling technology.

Environmental considerations are paramount as offshore drilling can pose risks to the marine ecosystem, including oil spills and disruptions to marine life by the noise and pollution. Advances in technology and stricter regulations have been aimed at minimizing the environmental impact of these operations. Meanwhile, decommissioned platforms sometimes find new life as artificial reefs, providing habitats for marine life and thus contributing to environmental conservation efforts.

These offshore structures vary greatly in design, ranging from towering fixed platforms anchored to the seabed to floating setups like TLPs (Tension-leg platforms) and spars, which are stabilized by mooring lines. Each design choice is influenced by water depth, environmental factors, and specific operational needs. As technology advances and the demand for resources grows, the designs and methods of offshore extraction continue to evolve, pushing the boundaries of what is possible in oil and gas extraction.

### 7.3.3 Marine Navigation

Marine navigation, the art and science of steering a ship from one point to another, integrates both skill and comprehensive knowledge. It requires understanding of physical, mathematical, oceanographic, cartographic, and astronomical principles to navigate seas efficiently and safely. The term "navigation" comes from the Latin word "navigatio", meaning the act of sailing or voyaging, while "nautical" and "naval" relate to the skills and aspects of navigating ships, particularly within the navy.

Throughout history, marine navigation has played a crucial role in trade, exploration, and cultural exchange. For example, ancient civilizations like the Egyptians and Phoenicians mastered navigation for trading and establishing routes across the Mediterranean and beyond. These early navigators relied on stars like the North Star atnight and the sun during the day to guide their voyages. Maritime exploits were not without conflict; the first recorded naval battle took place around 1210 BC between the Hittites and Cyprus.

Advancements in navigation technology over the centuries have significantly shaped human history. The invention of the compass, believed to have been introduced to Europe through the Arabs who acquired it from the Chinese, was pivotal. This, along with other navigational aids like the astrolabe and sextant, spurred the Age of Discovery. This era saw explorers like Christopher Columbus in 1492 and Vasco de Gama in 1498 undertaking voyages that connected continents.

The methods of navigation have evolved from observing celestial bodies to sophisticated electronic systems. Modern navigation utilizes technologies such as GPS and other satellite navigation systems, which are the most commonly used today due to their ease of use and accuracy. Inertial navigation systems, which analyze data from accelerometers and gyroscopes, further enhance a ship's ability to determine its location accurately.

In summary, marine navigation is a crucial discipline that combines ancient techniques and modern technology to guide ships across the world's oceans safely and effectively. Its development over the millennia has been integral to global exploration, trade, and cultural exchange.

## 7.3.4 Underwater Acoustics

Underwater acoustics, also known as hydroacoustics, involves the study of how sound behaves in water. It examines the interactions between sound waves and the water, its contents, and its boundaries. This field is both an art and a science—it requires the navigator skills to maneuver through the marine environment safely and is grounded in various scientific disciplines like physics, mathematics, and oceanography.

Underwater acoustic propagation is a complex process influenced by various factors that transform sound waves through refraction, reflection, and scattering. The behavior of sound waves in water is determined by the speed gradients of sound in the water. Notably, vertical gradients generally have a greater influence than horizontal ones. As depth increases, the pressure in the ocean also increases, which in turn raises the speed of sound, leading to a reversal in the sound speed gradient at the thermocline. This reversal creates an efficient waveguide at a particular depth where the sound speed reaches its minimum.

This variation in sound speed profiles leads to distinct regions in the water. For instance, "Shadow Zones" are areas with low sound intensity, whereas "Caustics" are regions where sound intensity is high. Scientists employ ray tracing methods to locate these zones and to understand their properties. In equatorial and temperate regions, where surface temperatures are higher, the pressure effects are reversed, forming a sound speed minimum at several hundred meters depth. This results in the creation of the deep sound channel, or SOFAR channel, which allows sounds to travel thousands of kilometers without interacting with the sea surface or the seabed.

Additionally, in the deep sea, convergence zones form where sound waves are bent downward from near-surface sources and then back upwards again, dependent on the sound speed gradients. Similarly, in both deep and moderately shallow waters, a phenomenon known as a surface duct can occur when there is upward refraction caused by cold surface temperatures, allowing sound to propagate by bouncing repeatedly off the water's surface.

Understanding these underwater acoustic propagation phenomena is crucial for various applications including sonar systems, communication, and environmental monitoring within the dynamic ocean environment. This understanding is further enhanced by tools like hydrophones, similar to underwater microphones, which measure pressure fluctuations caused by sound waves in water. These measurements are critical, providing insights about sound pressure levels and the spectral density of sound, thus allowing a deeper understanding of underwater acoustics. This knowledge is essential not just for navigation and sonar applications but also plays a significant role in marine research and conservation efforts, helping to balance human activities with the preservation of marine ecosystems.

Underwater acoustics involves a range of specialized devices that play crucial roles in marine navigation, communication, and research. Among these devices, hydrophones are fundamental. Acting as underwater microphones, they detect sound waves in water, making them essential for acoustic data collection across various applications, including environmental monitoring and submarine warfare.

Sonar systems are another pivotal technology in underwater acoustics. Active sonar systems emit sound pulses and listen for echoes, which help determine the location, speed, and other characteristics of underwater objects or terrain. In contrast, passive sonar systems do not emit signals but listen to sounds produced by marine phenomena, making them especially useful in military operations for stealth monitoring.

The Acoustic Doppler Current Profiler (ADCP) is instrumental in oceanographic research. By utilizing the Doppler effect, it measures variations in water current speeds and directions, which is crucial for understanding ocean currents that affect climate patterns and marine ecology. Autonomous Underwater Vehicles (AUVs), equipped with sonar and other sensors, autonomously conduct detailed mappings of the ocean floor, aiding in discoveries such as historical shipwrecks and studying deep-sea environments.

Underwater acoustic modems facilitate wireless data transmission underwater by converting digital information into sound waves, enabling communication between submerged equipment, divers, and surface stations. SOFAR spheres, which utilize the deep sound channel to detect acoustic events across vast distances, were originally developed to locate downed pilots during World War II but are now used in scientific studies to monitor global whale populations.

Additionally, specialized underwater microphones, designed to record the sounds of marine life, are used extensively in bioacoustics research. These devices offer high sensitivity and a broad frequency range, suitable for capturing a variety of acoustic signals from species like whales and dolphins.

Together, these devices showcase the diverse technology used in underwater acoustics, each enhancing our understanding and interaction with the complex underwater world. They are invaluable in advancing marine research, conservation efforts, and our sustainable use of ocean resources.

## 7.3.5 Naval Ships

A naval ship, also known as a naval vessel, is a military ship or sometimes a boat, used by a navy for various purposes. Unlike civilian ships, naval ships are built to be resilient and are typically equipped with weaponry, although armament on troop transports may be light or nonexistent. Designed primarily for naval warfare, these ships are often called warships, distinguishing them from support vessels or those used for shipyard operations.

The classification of naval ships varies, with no universal agreement. Key classes include aircraft carriers, which are essentially mobile airfields designed to conduct combat operations by the carrier-based aircraft. Surface combatants encompass various heavily armed ships like battleships and cruisers, designed to engage enemy forces at sea. Submarines, whether used for combat or other purposes, operate submerged and have some level of combat capability. Patrol combatants have extended endurance for operations beyond coastal duties, while amphibious warfare ships support amphibious assaults.

Other classifications include combat logistics ships that provide replenishment to fleet units and mine warfare ships designated for mine-related operations. Coastal defense ships focus on patrol and interdiction near shorelines, and sealift ships support long-range material transport. Support vessels help with general tasks across open oceans, and service type craft provide general support close to shore or to other naval operations.

In terms of size, naval ships range from large aircraft carriers and helicopter carriers to smaller frigates, corvettes, and patrol boats. The classification often depends on the ship's role, tonnage, and technological capabilities, with many of the larger vessels considered capital ships.

Navies also utilize auxiliary ships for non-combat roles such as transport and logistical support. These include ammunition ships, barracks ships for temporary accommodation, colliers in the Age of Steam, and command ships that serve as a fleet commander's flagship. Hospital ships offer medical treatment at sea, complying with international laws that protect them during conflict. Repair ships, including those specialized for aircraft or submarines, provide necessary maintenance. Other auxiliary types include rescue and salvage ships, research vessels for military research, replenishment oilers for refueling, and intelligence gathering ships for intelligence gathering.

Each class of ship plays a vital role in the operational capabilities of a navy, from direct combat operations and troop deployment to logistical support and training. The diversity in ship types allows navies to project power, conduct surveillance, support marine operations, and ensure readiness for various maritime operations.

APPLY YOUR KNOWLEDGE

1. What are the emerging trends in blue biotechnology and how might they impact the sustainable development of ocean resources, including potential ethical considerations and the balance between commercial exploitation and conservation efforts?

2. With the retreat of Arctic sea ice due to climate change, how can the increased navigability of Arctic shipping routes be leveraged for economic and transportation efficiency while ensuring the protection of the fragile Arctic environment, and what international shipping regulations need to be established to address potential environmental impacts?

## AFTER CLASS

### KEY TERMS

| | | |
|---|---|---|
| Ocean governance | NATO | Underwater acoustics |
| UNCLOS | APEC | Aircraft carrier |
| IMO | Arctic Council | Naval architecture |

### EXTENSION

■ Sea Warfare Changes and the Evolution of Naval Technology

Naval technology has drastically changed over time, transforming how battles are fought at sea.

In ancient times, simple ships powered by oars and sails were used in battles. Civilizations like the Greeks and Romans used ships such as triremes, which had three rows of oars and were designed for ramming enemy vessels.

From the 16th to the 19th centuries, naval warfare entered the Age of Sail. Ships grew larger and carried multiple cannons. The tactic of lining up ships to fire broadsides became common. Notable battles during this time included those of the Napoleonic Wars.

The 19th century introduced steam-powered ships and ironclads. These ships, like the USS Monitor and CSS Virginia, had iron armor and steam engines, making them more resilient and maneuverable. This period marked a significant change in naval tactics.

In the early 20th century, the Dreadnought revolutionized naval warfare. These battleships had uniform heavy guns and steam turbines, making older ships obsolete. During World War II, aircraft carriers began to replace battleships as the main force at sea, as seen in the Pearl Harbor attack.

Today, aircraft carriers are the centerpieces of modern navies, capable of launching aircraft for various missions. Submarines, especially nuclear-powered ones, are crucial for stealth and deterrence. Modern warships are also equipped with guided missiles and advanced defense systems like the Aegis Combat System.

Recent advancements include unmanned systems like drones and autonomous underwater vehicles (AUVs) for surveillance and mine-clearing. Stealth technology, as seen in Zumwalt-class destroyers, helps ships avoid detection. Cyber warfare capabilities have also become important for defending against electronic threats.

Naval technology has come a long way, from ancient oar-powered ships to advanced modern warships. Each technological breakthrough has changed how battles are fought at sea, shaping the tactics and strategies of naval warfare today. Understanding these changes highlights the complexity and innovation in modern maritime combat.

CASE STUDY

■ The Arctic-Strategic Significance and the Current Geopolitical Situation

The Arctic region is becoming increasingly important due to its vast resources, new shipping routes, and geopolitical interests.

1. Strategic Significance

The Arctic is rich in natural resources, including significant amounts of oil, natural gas, and minerals. Melting ice is making these resources more accessible. Additionally, new shipping routes like the Northern Sea Route and the Northwest Passage are opening up, significantly shortening travel times between Europe and Asia, which offers economic benefits but also environmental and navigational challenges.

2. Balance of Power

Russia has the longest Arctic coastline and a significant military and economic presence. It invests heavily in Arctic infrastructure and aims to control the Northern Sea Route and exploit its resources.

The United States focuses on national security, economic opportunities, and environmental protection in the Arctic. While it has been slower to develop its Arctic infrastructure compared to Russia, it is increasing its focus on the region.

Canada emphasizes sovereignty, sustainable development, and environmental stewardship. Canada claims the Northwest Passage as internal waters and invests in Arctic infrastructure to assert its sovereignty.

Norway balances resource exploitation with environmental protection and has significant economic interests in the Barents Sea. It actively participates in Arctic governance.

Denmark (Greenland) supports Greenland's greater autonomy while protecting Danish and Greenlandic interests. The U. S. military base in Thule, Greenland, is crucial for American defense strategy.

China, though not an Arctic state, has shown increasing interest in the region as a near-Arctic state. China's Arctic policy focuses on scientific research, resource exploration, and the development of new shipping routes, seeking to establish a presence in Arctic governance through investments and partnerships, emphasizingthe potential economic benefits of shorter shipping routes and access to untapped resources.

The Arctic Council promotes cooperation among Arctic states and Indigenous communities on sustainable development and environmental protection. UNCLOS provides a legal framework for resolving territorial and resource claims.

Environmental threats from climate change, increased shipping traffic, and potential geopolitical conflicts pose significant challenges. However, the Arctic also offers opportunities for international cooperation on climate change research, sustainable development, and disaster response.

The Arctic's strategic importance is growing due to its resources and new shipping routes. The balance of power involves complex interactions between Arctic and non-Arctic states, each pursuing their own interests. Understanding these dynamics is crucial for anticipating future developments and promoting cooperative approaches to manage the region's challenges and opportunities.

CLASS DISCUSSION

How can the international community balance the strategic, economic, and environmental interests in the Arctic region to ensure sustainable development and regional stability, while addressing the growing geopolitical tensions and environmental challenges posed by climate change?

FOR FUN

1. Website to visit

(1) 101 Sublime Facts about the Ocean. FactRetriever. com

(2) Woods Hole Oceanographic Institution (whoi. edu): a wealth of information on ocean research, technology, and educational resources.

2. Book to read

张宏声. 中国参与全球海洋治理的理念与实践

张宏声,中国太平洋学会会长,原国家海洋局副局长、党组成员、保密委员会主任。

# Unit 8 Regions in Global Context: Global Governance

This is global governance in the making. But we must agree, and agree to a binding commitment.

—George Papandreou

## LEARNIING OUTCOMES

■ Describe the evolution and significance of global governance theory, especially in the context of China's involvement and contribution.

■ Recognize the key principles and mechanisms that guide global governance practices.

■ Understand the complexities and evolving nature of the world order, including the major forces and ideologies that have shaped it and those that are driving its transformation.

■ Analyze the impact of China's Belt and Road Initiative (BRI) on global financial governance and infrastructure development.

## BEFORE CLASS

■ Jin Nuo. Future and Responsibility: Perspectives on China's Role in Global Governance. Foreign Languages Press, 2019.

■ Alice D. Ba and Matthew J. Hoffmann, eds. Contending Perspectives on Global Governance: Coherence, contestation and world order. Routledge (Taylor & Francis Group) London and New York, 2005.

After you read the above materials, please answer the following questions.

1. How do you understand the concepts and definitions of global governance?

2. How do you understand the changes in world order?

3. How do you understand the new international relations?
4. How do you understand China's role in the reform of global financial system?
5. How do you understand the function of BRI in global governance?

## 8.1 Theory and Concept of Global Governance

The term "governance" began to rise in prominence within Western scholarly circles in the 1990s. A critical factor driving the popularity of this term was the advent of a new phase of globalization following the conclusion of the Cold War, which brought about significant transformations in the political and social fabric of societies. Among these changes was a fundamental shift from traditional political rule to a new model of governance at the heart of human societal and political spheres. This shift involved moving away from government-driven rule towards governance without the need for central governments, and from national governance to a global governance framework.

The necessity for global governance stems from various scholarly perspectives: Some argue that the emergence of a global marketplace due to economic globalization necessitates the creation of an entity responsible for the global oversight and coordination. Others suggest that the Information Age has led to unequal and insufficient information exchange across countries, warranting the establishment of international cooperation and coordination mechanisms. Additionally, some academics have posited that global governance is essential as a response to the rise and exacerbation of worldwide issues.

Following the introduction of the global governance concept, scholars and research institutions worldwide have explored this idea through various lenses and contributed to the theoretical design of global governance systems. Different international organizations have also released studies and proposed diverse strategies. In 1995, notable global figures including former German Chancellor Willy Brandt and former Swedish Prime Minister Ingvar Carlsson, under the auspices of the United Nations, founded the Commission on Global Governance. This body released a report titled "*Our Global Neighborhood*" in celebration of the United Nations' 50th anniversary, which highlighted the concept's importance. One of the earliest academic efforts to define global governance was by American scholar Lawrence Finkelstein, who described it as a form of governance without sovereign authority, managing relationships that extend beyond national borders. This form of governance parallels the functions of domestic governments on an international scale. Scholar Jim Whitman later identified six core definitions of global governance, including its role in international organizations, as a mix of state and non-state activities, and as a mechanism for managing specific global areas and issues.

Chinese scholars have also been closely monitoring and contributing to the global governance discourse since the mid-1990s. Prominent intellectuals like YuKeping and Cai Tuo have authored numerous works on this critical topic in international politics. According to Yu, global governance encompasses five principal elements: its values, rules, actors, objeitives, and outcomes. The values of global governance represent the aspirations and objectives that must be pursued globally, transcending national, racial, religious, ideological, and socio-economic differences. The rules are designed to preserve the normal order of the international community and to achieve the espoused values. These include international principles, norms, standards, policies, agreements, and procedures, which are fundamental to global governance.

The actors involved in global governance include organizations responsible for developing and implementing global rules. These actors consist of governments at various levels, formal international organizations such as the United Nations (UN), the World Bank, and the World Trade Organization (WTO), as well as informal global civil society organizations. The targets of global governance are the transnational issues that impact multiple countries or humanity as a whole, which no single nation can resolve independently and which therefore require the collaborative efforts of the international community. The outcomes of global governance are critical for evaluating its effectiveness, primarily reflected through the performance of international rules.

While the theory of global governance has been extensively discussed in academic circles globally, its practical application, particularly in Western contexts, has faced challenges. The rise of anti-globalization sentiments and the continuous emergence of global problems suggest that the existing frameworks of global governance are struggling to address and resolve these issues effectively. In this changing geopolitical landscape, China's power is rapidly ascending, there is an increasing need for China to engage more deeply in global governance. Moreover, China is called upon to proactively offer its insights and solutions to address global challenges, contributing what is often referred to as "Chinese wisdom" to the international community. This involvement is seen as crucial for enhancing the efficacy and relevance of global governance in today's complex world.

APPLY YOUR KNOWLEDGE

1. How does the concept of global governance challenge the traditional sovereignty of nation-states, and what role does China play in reshaping this concept?

2. Considering the criticisms and challenges faced by global governance structures, what improvements or innovations could potentially enhance the effectiveness of global governance mechanisms, particularly in managing global crises like pandemics or climate change?

# 8.2 Changes in World Order

## 8.2.1 What is World Order?

The topic of "world order" has gained renewed interest due to significant shifts occurring globally. Discussions on this topic, both locally and internationally, prompt us to delve into its essential nature. What exactly comprises the world order? This question demands a theoretical examination, as suggested by Henry Kissinger in hisbook "*World Order*", where he provocatively claims that a real world order doesn't exist—a curious stance given the title of his work.

For many, the phrase "world order" might seem trite, similar to "international landscape". It's crucial to recognize that world order represents a fundamental concept in the theory of world politics. Without a thorough understanding of its theoretical underpinnings, any analysis of world order risks being superficial, merely cataloging events without grasping their deeper significance.

Analyzing world order effectively requires placing it within the broader context of world politics rather than merely examining inter-country relations. The complexity of world order goes beyond simple international dynamics. Western nations, often engaged in power struggles, significantly influenced the modern conception of world order through events like World War Ⅱ. This conflict led to a new global structure, which despite its ambiguities and the bipolar tension that followed the war, was predominantly shaped by Western ideologies, particularly the American-promoted "liberal world order".

This concept, rooted in the 19th century, gained further clarity post-Cold War, aligning with the "end of history" theory and the beliefs upheld by global elites at forums like Davos. These perspectives underscore the enduring impact and relevance of the liberal world order in contemporary geopolitical discussions.

## 8.2.2 The Values Shaping World Order

The term "liberal world order" signifies a post-World War Ⅱ international framework characterized by liberal democracy. This notion is rooted in a long history of liberal imperialism, notably marked by 200 years of British dominance from 1700 to 1900. The subsequent global conflicts, including the two World Wars from 1900 to 1945, were not fundamentally disputes over the essence of liberal imperialism but contests over leadership within this order. After World War Ⅱ, particularly post-Cold War, this liberal imperialistic framework explicitly evolved into what is now recognized as the liberal world order.

Western civilizations have long understood the profound influence of values on world order. Tracing back to the late Roman Empire era, Europeans have consistently lived under ideologically or religiously defined orders. For instance, the perpetual conflicts between differing religious ideologies spurred centuries of warfare, including the Crusades and intra-European conflicts such as France's religious wars, culminating in the *Peace of Westphalia*, which itself was a product of these extensive religious conflicts. These historical periods were not merely conflicts but were foundational in establishing the value-based systems that influenced future governance structures, including the ideological battles between liberalism and socialism that eventually led to the rise of fascism after liberalism's perceived failure in Europe.

The Cold War is another example of an ideological conflict, underpinning the significance of values in shaping global order. Hence, any discussion of world order that omits the influence of values is incomplete and neglects the historical essence of how global systems are formed and operated.

Contrastingly, the Chinese approach to world order has historically been less ideologically driven due to its secular politics from the pre-Qin period and a cultural emphasis on maintaining a respectful distance from religious or spiritual absolutes. This perspective offers a distinct framework, potentially less swayed by the ideological fervor that characterizes much of Western history. However, given the global nature of politics,

China too engages in a discourse of values-oriented world order, highlighting the universal relevance of values in shaping international relations and governance structures.

### 8.2.3 Understanding the International System

The international system is a complex framework composed of both formal and informal institutions, norms, international conventions, and various global organizations. This system, primarily founded on the principles of the *Treaty of Westphalia*, was significantly shaped and expanded after World War Ⅱ. It encompasses key political and economic structures such as the United Nations, and financial institutions like the World Bank and the International Monetary Fund. Additionally, global economic organizations such as the World Trade Organization (WTO) play a critical role in this system.

International conventions and multilateral treaties are integral components of the international system, facilitating cooperation and standardization across nations. However, international norms, which guide these conventions and treaties, often become points of contention. A pertinent example is the debate over whether human rights should override national sovereignty, which could justify interventions in a country's internal politics, or if the sanctity of national sovereignty should prevail over human rights considerations.

The establishment and interpretation of these international norms are largely influenced by the dominant countries within the system. These nations often shape the discourse and policies according to their strategic interests and ideological leanings, impacting the overall dynamics and effectiveness of the international system.

The international system has been influenced by dominant states, often referred to as "system suppliers", since the 18th century. These states have not only provided the structure but have also imbued the system with specific value orientations. Consequently, the effectiveness of the world order and the international system heavily relies on the governance capabilities and attributes of these dominating states. However, this doesn't exclude the possibility of achieving consensus with less influential nations.

World order can be understood as having two components: the values underpinning the existing structure and the dynamic governance capabilities of major countries. Furthermore, the present form of the status quo is dependent on how these major countries manage and adapt to changes.

Understanding the governance abilities of these dominant nations in the context of change is crucial for explaining the evolution of world order. Without this insight, one cannot accurately describe or analyze the world order during periods of transition.

It's important to recognize that this analysis is a product of apartícular approach to global politics, which views international relations through the lens of domestic and comparative politics. This perspective asserts that a thorough discussion of world order must be rooted in the broader context of world politics rather than confined to the interactions between major powers. The latter approach often falls short in capturing the complexities and nuances of the world order.

## 8.2.4 The Evolution of the Current World Order

The historical narrative of the current world order can be traced back to significant epochs, but a focused analysis might begin around 1700 CE, a period marking the onset of profound changes in global dynamics. Prior to this, while global interactions existed, they lacked the defined structure and dominant values characteristic of a "world order". The Industrial Revolution, particularly in Britain, catalyzed the ascendance of Western powers and shaped global politics significantly.

1. The Formation of the Western-led World Order

Understanding the Western-led world order requires examining the evolution of Western nation-states, fundamentally shaped by trade and war. These two elements not only defined the nature of nation-states but also laid the groundwork for global dominance.

2. Economic-Military Influence

From the mid-17th to the mid-19th century, European nations solidified their domestic political structures, predominantly under capitalist influences, which then extended outward through colonial expansion. This period saw the bourgeoisie consolidate power domestically, aligning with overseas trade and colonial conquests. A pivotal moment in this outward expansion was the Berlin Conference of 1884—1885, which formalized the division of Africa among European powers. The subsequent World Wars were more about dominance within Europe rather than altering the global colonial framework, which remained largely intact until the decolonization movements from 1945 to 1975.

3. Political-Cultural Dominance

Alongside military and economic dominance, political and cultural ideologies also played crucial roles. The latter half of the 19th century witnessed the rise of social Darwinism, which provided a pseudo-scientific basis for colonialism and the supposed superiority of Western culture. Figures like Alexis de Tocqueville and John Stuart Mill justified European colonialism using arguments embedded in social Darwinist thought. Even during World War Ⅰ, German intellectuals like Max Weber attributed Western dominance to cultural factors, notably Protestant ethics.

4. Post-World War Theories and Institutional Dominance

After World War Ⅱ, and more distinctly after the Cold War, the concept of the "end of history" emerged, suggesting that liberal democracy represents the ultimate and most superior form of human governance. This ideology not only shaped global political discourse but also influenced U. S. foreign security strategies, reinforcing the belief in institutional superiority.

5. The Modern International System

The current international system is a complex interplay of economic, military, ideological, and political powers, as developed over three centuries. This system, underpinned by Western historical developments, was solidified with the establishment of international organizations and norms post-World War Ⅱ, creating a structured global order that reflects these long-standing influences. This structure not only dictates the governance capabilities of major nations but also shapes the interactions and policies that govern international relations today.

### 8.2.5 The Turbulence of the Liberal World Order and Emerging Shifts

The "liberal world order" that dominated global politics post-Cold War era saw the United States at the helm, symbolizing a time often characterized as "peace under U. S. governance". This period, regarded as an era of unchallenged American supremacy, coincided with widespread acceptance of the "end of history" thesis, which posited that liberal democracy was the ultimate form of government. However, significant events have challenged this order and its underlying principles.

1. Impact of the 2008 Financial Crisis and Arab Spring

The financial crisis of 2008, coupled with the political upheavals of the Arab Spring, severely undermined the credibility and stability of the liberal world order. These events highlighted vulnerabilities and inconsistencies within the system that the very architects of the order struggled to manage, leading to a perception of the builders turning into its destroyers.

2. Failure of Color Revolutions

The concept of "soft power", popularized by Joseph Nye, suggested that American values and governance models had universal appeal. This notion was tested through initiatives like the Greater Middle East Initiative (GMEI) and support for Color Revolutions, aimed at spreading democratic governance through non-coercive means. However, the outcomes were often counterproductive, leading to destabilization and governance crises in regions like the Middle East and Ukraine. These failures have diminished the allure of liberal democracy and questioned its efficacy as a universal model.

3. The Trump Administration's Impact on Global Governance

The President Trump's first tenure marked a significant departure from previous U. S. foreign policy approaches, particularly his skepticism towards multilateralism and global cooperation. His actions, such as withdrawing from the Paris Agreement, TPP, and the Iran nuclear deal, and threatening trade wars, signaled a broader American retreat from international commitments and liberal values. This shift has raised questions about the reliability of the U. S. as a global leader and its commitment to the liberal world order it once championed.

4. Rise of Non-Western Economies

The ascendance of economies like China has dramatically altered the global economic landscape. China's rise, in particular, represents a shift from the historical dominance of Western manufacturing and economic prowess. This change not only challenges the economic supremacy of the West but also introduces new cultural and political dynamics into the world order. China's development model, which emphasizes growth without reliance on war or colonial exploitation, presents a stark contrast to the paths historically taken by Western powers.

APPLY YOUR KNOWLEDGE

1. How can the world order adapt to ensure more equitable power distribution among emerging economies and established Western powers?

2. What role do cultural and ideological differences play in shaping conflicts and cooperation in the current world order?

## AFTER CLASS

### KEY TERMS

| | |
|---|---|
| Global Governance | Belt and Road Initiative(BRI) |
| World Order | Sovereignty |
| Mutual Respect | Win-Win Cooperation |
| Multilateralism | Community with a Shared Future for Mankind |
| Multipolarity | |

### EXTENSION

■ GLOBAL CATASTROPHIC RISKS 2024

Managing risks through collective action

2024: Overshadowed by intersecting global risks and a global governance architecture that is not fit for purpose, a new year offers new chances. Now it is up to us if we take them. We should look into the risks at stake and explore how we can approach a comprehensive overhaul of global governance to address them.

Among risks that threaten our societies, this year's report focuses on three of the most prominent—climate change, ecological collapse, and weapons of mass destruction. It examines how they have each developed, but also how they interact and exacerbate one another. For example, resource scarcity driven by climate change can spark conflict. Rising sea levels and more frequent extreme weather events also threaten the safety of nuclear facilities. When climate and environment intertwine with peace and security, we need a paradigm shift in multilateral cooperation.

The stark reality, underscored by our contributors, is that time is not on our side.

We stand close to crossing six of the nine planetary boundaries that define a safe operating space for humanity. Moreover, when we factor in "safe and just" limits—considering both Earth's stability and human welfare—the situation is even more threatening.

The pathway to effective global governance demands a dual strategy: immediate pragmatic actions and visionary, "blue-sky" thinking. For instance, when considering how to address the global governance of nuclear risk, it is important to both support the immediate work of the International Campaign to Abolish Nuclear Weapons (ICAN) and to get more states to sign up to the ban.

However, it's not just about policy; it's also about inclusivity. We must bring more people affected by global risks into the conversation. Civil society must be included in policy making to protect ecosystems, and non-nuclear states must be included in non-proliferation discussions. Only by amplifying diverse voices can we engineer solutions that have legitimacy and resonate universally.

The clock is ticking—yet it is not too late. Meaningful steps have been taken and can be taken again. The Earth, with its built-in resilience, presents us with an opportunity—a chance for humanity to reconstruct our collaborative endeavors and forge a safer world.

## CLASS DISCUSSION

According to you, how can we manage the catastrophic risks through new global governance?

## CASE STUDY

### ■ Zhou Xiaochuan and China's Role in Global Financial Governance

Zhou Xiaochuan served as the Governor of the People's Bank of China (PBOC) from 2002 to 2018, becoming the longest-serving head of China's central bank. His tenure is notable for the substantial reforms in China's financial system and its integration into the global financial architecture. Under Zhou's leadership, the key objectives were to modernize and liberalize China's financial sector, manage the country's monetary policy effectively during times of global financial stress, and increase China's influence in global financial governance.

Zhou implemented several significant reforms aimed at liberalizing China's financial markets, including:

①Promoting the international use of the Chinese yuan, ultimately leading to its inclusion in the IMF's Special Drawing Rights (SDR) basket in 2016.

②Overseeing the gradual liberalization of interest rates and the renminbi (RMB) exchange rate.

③Expanding the scope of the Shanghai and Shenzhen stock exchanges, improving China's capital markets'regulatory framework.

These measures have exerted great impact on global governance.

1. Renminbi Internationalization

Zhou advocated for the broader use of the RMB in international transactions, which was part of a broader strategy to reflect China's growing economic clout on the global stage. This move was also aimed at reducing China's dependency on the US dollar and thus its vulnerability to external shocks.

2. Global Financial Stability

During the 2008 financial crisis, Zhou played a crucial role in stabilizing China's economy and contributed to global efforts to manage the crisis. His policies helped maintain China's economic growth, which was crucial for global economic stability, given the slowdown in other major economies.

3. Influence in Global Financial Institutions

Zhou's leadership helped elevate China's voice in international financial institutions such as the International Monetary Fund (IMF) and the World Bank, advocating for greater representation for China and other emerging economies.

CLASS DISCUSSION

What kind of challenges is China's financial system facing in the process of its integration into the global financial architecture? What are the strategic implications of Zhou Xiaochuan's approach to integrating China more deeply into global financial governance? Analyze how individual leadership can influence a country's approach to global governance?

FOR FUN

1. Websites to visit

https://ggin.stimson.org/2024-un-civil-society-conference/

2. Movie to see

*The Big Short*(2015)

"*The Big Short*" is a book by Michael Lewis that was later adapted into a feature film. It details the build-up of the housing and credit bubble during the 2000s that led to the financial crisis of 2007—2008. The story follows several key figures who predicted the collapse and bet against the US mortgage market, thus profiting from the financial disaster.

3. Article to read

江时学, 论全球治理的必要性、成效及前景

江时学,上海大学特聘教授、拉美研究中心主任,察哈尔学会高级研究员,中国拉丁美洲学会顾问,中国新兴经济体研究会副会长。